EAST RIDING AIRFIELDS
1915-1920

EAST RIDING AIRFIELDS

1915-1920

GEOFFREY SIMMONS

FLIGHT
RECORDER
PUBLICATIONS

A passion for accuracy

First published in Great Britain in 2009 by
Crécy Publishing

© text Geoffrey Simmons

Digital photography and scanning by
Eduard Winkler

Colour artwork by
Peter Green

Maps by
Steve Longland

ISBN 9 780954 560591

Printed in China

Crécy Publishing Limited
1a Ringway Trading Estate
Shadowmoss Road
Manchester M22 4LH
www.crecy.co.uk

CONTENTS

DEDICATION

This is a small acknowledgement of the bravery and expertise of the men who flew the primitive machines of the time, often in appalling weather at night. It was from these early days that our modern air forces, aviation industry, aerial navigation aids and skills have developed.

It is also dedicated to my wife Audrey who has put up with my interest in boring old aeroplanes and even more boring deserted and decrepit old aerodromes.

ACKNOWLEDGEMENTS

Much of this document is based on the research by the author in the preparation of a book on the history of RAF Driffield, (*Strong Foundations* by the author and Barry Abraham, published in 2001). I am indebted to Dr Stephen Harrison for the details of land requisitions relating to RFC Eastburn and RAF Driffield in 1916 and the 1930s, his local knowledge and relevant detail from the results of his archaeological surveys in the area of Eastburn Farm/RFC Eastburn; Mr P Roworth of Driffield for his letter listing the American units there, based on his enquiries at the US National Archives; Stewart Leslie for his support and allowing me access over many years to the vast JMB/GSL Collection of First World War aeroplane photographs, prior to the collection going to the Fleet Air Arm Museum; Cec Mowthorpe for his photographs of Lowthorpe and Arthur Credland of Hull Maritime Museum for the use of photographs showing bomb damage to the city. Finally my thanks must go to Barry Ketley for his additional material and editorship and to whom all credit must go for the final appearance of this book.

GLOSSARY

Ranks and equivalents

Navy

German	British
Kptlt Kapitänleutnant	Lt Cdr Lieutenant Commander
Kvkpt Korvettenkapitän	Cdr Commander
Fregattenkapitän	Capt Captain

RFC	Royal Flying Corps
2nd Lt	Second Lieutenant
Lt	Lieutenant
Capt	Captain
Maj	Major
Lt Col	Lieutenant-Colonel

RNAS	Royal Naval Air Service
Sqn Cdr	Squadron Commander
Flt Cdr	Flight Commander
Flt Lt	Flight Lieutenant
Obs Lt	Observer Lieutenant
Flt Sub-Lt	Flight Sub-Lieutenant
Obs Sub-Lt	Observer Sub-Lieutenant
LM	Leading Mechanic

Abbreviations

Airco	Aircraft Manufacturing Company
AW	Sir W.G. Armstrong Whitworth and Company
BE	Blériot Experimental. Series of aeroplanes designed and developed at the Royal Aircraft Factory.
CO	Commanding Officer
DH	Aircraft developed by Airco and designed by Geoffrey de Havilland.
FK	Frederick Koolhoven, Dutch chief designer for Armstrong Whitworth.
ft	feet
in	inch
HD	Home Defence
hp	horse power
HQ	Head Quarters
L	German navy rigid airships built by Luftschiffbau-Zeppelin GmbH.
lb	pound (weight)
LZ	German army rigid airships built by Luftschiffbau-Zeppelin GmbH.
mph	miles per hour
MT	Mechanical or Motor Transport
NCO	Non-Commissioned Officer
NER	North Eastern Railway
RAF	Royal Aircraft Factory, after June 1918 known as the Royal Aircraft Establishment.
RAF	Royal Air Force.
SE	Scout Experimental
SL	German army rigid airships built by Luftschiffbau Schütte-Lanz.
Sqn	Squadron
TDS	Training Depot Station
TS	Training Squadron
USAAS	United States Army Air Service
USNFC	United States Naval Flying Corps
WRAF	Women's Royal Air Force
W/T	Wireless/Telegraphy
yd	yard

Time

The 24 hour clock is used for all times. Times given are in British Time ie Greenwich Mean Time, prior to the introduction of British Summer Time on 21 May 1916, when clocks were put forward one hour and used from March to October thereafter.

INTRODUCTION
Some corner of an English field

My interest in the aerodromes[1] of the First World War began when I was involved with the Blackburn Beverley, then at the Museum of Army Transport in Beverley. I was looking into the squadron histories of the units that had operated the Beverley and found that No 47 Squadron had been formed at Beverley in 1916. Looking further into this led me into the research of other aerodromes and landing grounds and the associated military aviation activities in the area during the First World War.

The existence of military airfields in the East Riding of Yorkshire from the 1939-45 conflict is well known. In fact most of the airfields built during the 'Expansion Period' of the Royal Air Force in the mid-1930s still survive in their original state. Many of the war time 'Emergency' airfields of the 1940s used for heavy bomber bases that had three paved runways, and sometimes up to three large hangars, however, have now disappeared, having been 'returned to agriculture', apart from a few obvious wartime

military buildings scattered around the sites that have been utilised by the local farmers.

Any visible evidence in the area of military aerodromes from the First World War has now mostly disappeared and there are now very few people who have memories of this period. Fortunately many records exist in archive documents and other authors' writings, although the latter in most cases have to be searched to extract specific details relating to this area. Two societies, *The International Cross & Cockade Society,* an association of First World War aviation historians and *The Airfield Research Group* (mainly Second World War) provide valuable research support.

This work is offered in an attempt to bring published information together, in some cases to correct early assumptions, and bring into the public arena hitherto unrecorded facts.

M G Simmons
Beverley, 2006
Member Airfield Research Group and Cross & Cockade International Society

[1] A now archaic word to describe small airfields or airports. It is used in the present work as it was contemporary with the period described.

The present putting green area to the west of the café at Hornsea Mere was once the site of two fabric Bessoneau hangars.

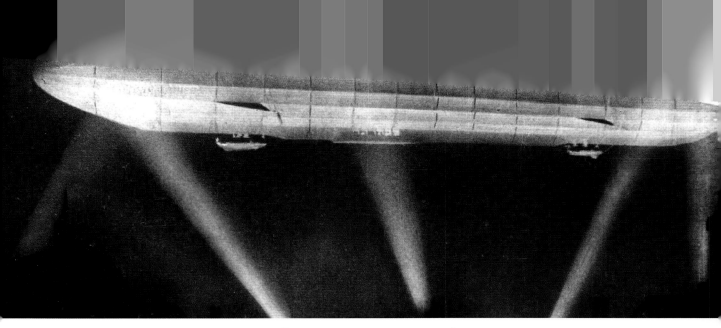

1 Background

At the beginning of the 1914-1918 war military air activity was rare; indeed, the aeroplane was still very much a novelty, for after all it was only 11 years since the Wright Brothers' experiments and while the aeroplane had advanced from the type of machines in the film *Those Magnificent Men In Their Flying Machines*, they were still crude devices.

An involvement with aviation activities in the East Riding of Yorkshire possibly began at Hedon in 1909 when a Hull marine engineer, Thomas Bell, designed and built a monoplane called Newington. It was reputed to have been taken out to the racecourse at Hedon where it was subsequently severely damaged after an encounter with a hedge. The machine never became airborne.

Engineer, inventor and motor garage owner Gordon Armstrong (Armstrong Shock Absorbers) had, on a visit to London in 1910, bought himself an aeroplane that was built from mainly Blériot parts. After assembling the machine and naming it on the tail, Armstrong No 1, he took it to Beverley Westwood twice to see if he, and it, could fly. On the second occasion he succeeded, albeit by only a few feet, the event being witnessed by a large crowd of local citizens and a reporter from the local paper.

During this period the Leeds engineer Robert Blackburn had been continuing his studies in Europe and during his stay in France had seen Wilbur Wright flying his primitive machine. He had also watched the early experiments of Latham, Blériot, Farman and other French pioneers. Bitten by the aviation bug, he returned to Leeds in 1908 to Thomas Green & Sons where his father was the works manager, determined to design, build and fly an aeroplane. He was not allowed to do this at Green's works but rented a workshop in Leeds and built his first monoplane. The machine was transported to Marske in a horse-drawn

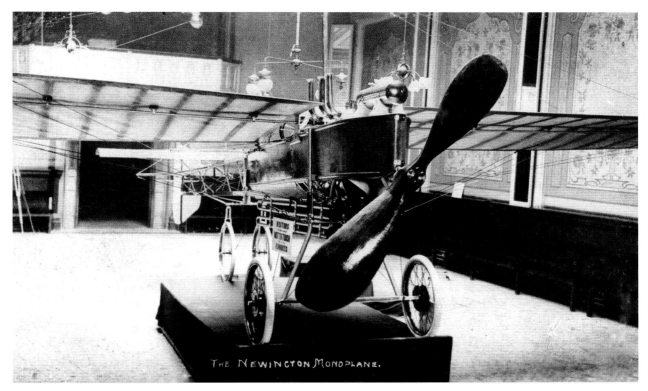

THE NEWINGTON MONOPLANE.

furniture van in April 1909. After many attempts to get airborne the machine was broken up in May 1910. Undeterred, he set about designing and building a more conventional aeroplane. In October of 1910 he rented a hangar and bungalow at Low Cliffs, Filey (at this time in the East Riding) that were owned and shared with Tranmer's Northern Automobile Co Ltd. who had opened the

'aerodrome' on 25 July 1910 and used Blériot machines to offer flying lessons. In addition to his own aviation activities Robert Blackburn repaired the Blériot machines in his Leeds workshop. The hangar was dismantled many years later, the roof trusses, support piers and the roof cladding were rebuilt in Hunmanby. The structure was still in use by an engineering company in the 1990s.

Above: Thomas Bell's Newington monoplane, presumably on display in the Town Hall in Hedon in 1909 or so. Despite the early date it boasts some remarkably advanced features, notably the monoplane layout. The designer's marine engineering background reveals itself in the boat-shaped fuselage and the propeller, worthy of a small yacht.

Left: Gordon Armstrong at the controls of his aircraft on Beverley Westwood. Believed to have been assembled from Blériot components, the machine is clearly not ready to fly as it has no wings, but has already been modified with the addition of a tailwheel and been named Armstrong No 1. The three-cylinder 35hp Anzani engine stood for many years until the 1950s in the corner of the car showroom of Armstrong's Garage in North Bar Within, Beverley.

The hangar for the Northern Aero Syndicate under construction on Low Cliffs at Filey. There was no mistaking its nationality.

Gustav Hamel in his Blériot monoplane visited the race course at Hedon where he spent four days in July 1912 giving exhibition flights from the former racecourse and visiting Preston, Sutton and Withernsea. Hamel was the first aviator to fly across the Humber, from Hedon to Grimsby, on 17 July.

During the Hornsea and District Horse and Foal Society Show on 12 June 1913, Stanley Adams brought his hydro-aeroplane Waterhen by road from Windermere and flew it from the Mere, giving demonstration and passenger flights over and along the shore line. The machine was operated by The Lakes Flying Company of Windermere. Some early float-planes had operated occasionally from the Mere, giving demonstrations and passenger flights prior to the outbreak of the 1914-18 conflict.

While this early civil aviation activity was entertaining and amazing many East Riding inhabitants, specific military aviation had not yet arrived in the area. The possibility of air bombardment, however, had been exercising the mind of governments for some years before the commencement of hostilities in 1914. The Hague Conference of 1899 had barred combatants from delivering projectiles or explosives from balloons or aerial devices. A second conference of 1907 further barred the

The completed hangar and three roomed bungalow rented from J W F Tranmer of Scarborough by Robert Blackburn for 10 shillings per week each. The Blériot Monoplane would indicate that this photograph was taken in the days of Tranmer's Northern Automobile Co Ltd.

Stanley Adams taxies the Waterhen on Hornsea Mere during the Hornsea and District Horse and Foal Show on 12 June 1913.

bombing of undefended places. In 1908 the British Government charged the Committee of Imperial Defence to study the threat posed by airships and aeroplanes and to advise the advantages that Britain could derive from their use. A sub-committee reported back that the airship, in addition to reconnaissance and the transport of small raiding parties, could be used to bomb ships and dockyards against which the defences would probably be inadequate.

In 1911 the Royal Flying Corps Military Wing and the Royal Flying Corps Naval Wing had each formed the beginnings of an air service using heavier-than-air machines, but Britain lagged behind other countries in this respect and in an attempt to remedy this situation the Committee of Imperial Defence proposed a unified air service. After the formation of the Royal Flying Corps by Royal Warrant in 1912 it became apparent that the ideas and philosophies of the two services were divergent. The Army tended to become bogged down with rules and regulations and considered that airborne devices provided enhanced reconnaissance and artillery spotting capability, whereas the Navy, more technically minded and with more money to spend, had a background of units operating remotely of their home bases.

The RFC Military Wing was required in August 1912 to provide aircraft to defend ports and other key objectives, such as London. The War Office, which considered the primary objective of its Military Wing of the RFC was the support of the Army on the battlefield,

failed to produce an air defence scheme, but the Admiralty started to establish aerodromes and a series of landing grounds around the British coastline intended mainly to protect its shore installations and support naval units by coastal patrols. These bases also had obvious value in the air defence of the east and south of Britain.

The interest in the 'lighter-than-air' devices by the pre-war Royal Flying Corps was divided between the Military Wing, in which the interest was in the balloon for battlefield spotting purposes, and the Royal Engineers who had experimented with small airships. The Naval Wing was interested in the maritime patrol capabilities of the airship and had ordered a rigid airship from the Vickers Company at Barrow-in-Furness. Unfortunately this machine broke its back before its first flight, and a Parseval airship was purchased from Germany for Admiralty experiments immediately prior to the outbreak of war.

On 1 July 1914 the RFC Naval Wing was reorganized as the Royal Naval Air Service under Admiralty control although it remained on paper part the Naval Wing RFC until 1 August 1915.

The RNAS established a naval air station at Killingholme on the Lincolnshire shore of the Humber estuary in July 1914 which had facilities for landplanes but in the main operated seaplanes and flying boats. An Air Acceptance Park was also established on the site.

By the outbreak of war in August 1914 the War Office still had no coherent home air defence policy and at the time was concentrating on providing air support for the British Expeditionary Force in France. Fortunately, in the early months of the war the Germans did not have the bases from which their aircraft could attack Britain and on 3 September 1914 the RNAS took over the responsibility for the air defence of Great Britain.

On 23 September a Short Improved S41 seaplane (s/n 20) was deployed to Bridlington by the Naval Wing RFC until the 27th. The unarmed aircraft, flown by Lt Courtney RN, operated from the beach using a custom made ramp to give access the sea.

The German army soon overran Belgium and captured coastal towns where bases were established that reduced the flying distances to targets in the south east of England. Preliminary attacks on Great Britain commenced in December 1914 and were carried out by Friedrichshafen FF 29 seaplanes from the German Navy *See-Flieger Abteilung* 1 (Seaplane Unit No 1), based at Zeebrugge. These attacks, by single machines, were against Dover and the Thames area in daylight. There were no casualties and only £40 worth of damage to property in Dover by a 22lb bomb.

The potential of the airship for offensive operations had been realised by the German authorities and their development of the rigid airship (generically known as the Zeppelin) went on apace. Subsequently, Zeppelin attacks against British towns commenced in 1915.

Three Zeppelins set out on the first bombing raid by an airship on the night of 19/20 January 1915. Two German Navy Zeppelins, L 3 and L 4, left Fuhlsbüttel (now Hamburg airport) to attack the Humber area and L 6 departed Nordholz (between Bremerhaven and Cuxhaven) intending to attack targets in the Thames estuary. L 6 turned back with engine trouble some ninety miles short of the English coast. L 3, commanded by *Kptlt* Hans Fritz, was carried by the wind to the south of his intended landfall consequently he decided to bomb Great Yarmouth, where he dropped six high explosive and seven incendiary bombs at 2025 hrs. *Kptlt* Magnus von Platen-Hallemund, commanding L4, was hopelessly lost and thought he was to the north of his target area. He claimed to have attacked fortified places between the Tyne and the Humber. In reality, he had scattered bombs over several Norfolk villages, overflown Sandringham and

dumped the remaining majority of his bomb load on undefended Kings Lynn. This first Zeppelin raid resulted in four killed, sixteen injured and £7,740 damage on the ground.

The M-class Zeppelins used on this raid were 518ft long, powered by three 210hp Maybach engines that produced a top speed of 52mph and the maximum ceiling was about 5,000ft with a bomb load of 1,100 to 1,430 lbs. Against these the RFC put up two sorties by Vickers FB5 aeroplanes from Joyce Green aerodrome (in Kent between Dartford and the river Thames). The Vickers FB5 'Gunbus' was a two-seat biplane in which the crew sat in tandem open cockpits; the observer with a Vickers machine-gun, in the nose to the front of the pilot. The Gunbus was powered by one 100hp Monosoupape rotary engine that had a reputation for being unreliable, mounted at the rear of the short cockpit pod with a pusher propeller. The maximum speed of the Gunbus was 70mph.

The commitment of the RFC to support the army on the Western Front with what at the time were inadequate resources put the onus for Home air defence on the Admiralty and the RNAS which were also stretched. Defence against air attack became a major concern of the Government and decisions were made to increase the number of units committed to air defence and the ground facilities to support them including landing grounds, as the original aerodromes were known.

As a result of this decision the land for the first military aerodrome in the East Riding was requisitioned. At a meeting of the Beverley Town Council held on 3 April 1915 a Council committee was advised that the Military Authorities intended to erect an aerodrome in the neighbourhood of the Hurn (the area of common pasture to the north of the York Road) which included the existing racecourse.

On the night of the 4/5 June 1915 a German rigid airship, the Navy Schütte-Lanz SL 3 (*Kptlt* Fritz Bömack), crossed the English coast ten miles south of Bridlington intending to attack the Humber area. Navigation had been hindered by the strong wind and poor visibility, such that by about 2300 hrs the Zeppelin was well off-course as it was seen in the vicinity of Driffield Parish Church. Mr Leggett of Driffeld remembers seeing this Zeppelin (as they were all generically called, although two manufacturers were involved in the production of these rigid airships, Schütte-Lanz and Luftschiff-Zeppelin) and recalls how slowly it appeared to be moving. SL 3 reached Flamborough Head at 0030 hrs and then set course for Hull. The intruder was still having problems with navigation as it was then reported to have cruised around in the area of Langtoft and Sledmere before passing over Driffield again at about 0100 hrs the next morning, 5 May, when two bombs were dropped on the town, one of which dropped about a hundred yards from Mr. Leggett's home and blew in all their windows. Apart from cuts from glass there were no serious casualties on the ground and the damage was restricted to broken glass. Boemack then abandoned the raid and returned to Germany. The RNAS and RFC mounted nine defence sorties from the aerodromes at Eastchurch, Grain, Joyce Green and Northolt, all in the southern counties, without success.

Two nights later the heaviest raid of the war to date took place on the night of the 6/7 June when Navy Zeppelin L 9 and Army Zeppelins LZ 37, LZ 38 and LZ 39 set out from their Belgian bases, primarily to attack London. All the Army Zeppelins, however, returned to base with engine and navigation troubles without reaching the English coast. Shortly after take-off *Kptlt* H. Mathy in L 9 decided to raid Hull. He made landfall near Cromer on the north Norfolk coast at 2000 hrs, crossed the Wash flying in a northerly direction, to be seen briefly over Mablethorpe and reached Bridlington at 2310 hrs. Having established his position, he set course for Hull which he reached at 0050 hrs. First dropping a flare to illuminate the target, Mathy then dropped thirteen high-explosive and fifty incendiary bombs, mainly on the old town, around Holy Trinity Church and to the west of the Town Docks. The only opposition to the raid came from the 4-inch guns of the small cruiser HMS *Adventure* that was in dock for repair at the time. Two anti-Zeppelin patrols (AZP) were flown by the RNAS at Yarmouth at 2020-2210 hrs and 02.25-0430 hrs without sighting L 9. During the period of the raid Killingholme was unable to mount a sortie as it was blanketed in fog. A Sopwith Two-seater Scout ('Spinning Jenny'),1055 hrs, managed to take off at 0510 hrs for a patrol but Mathy in L 9 had long departed. The raid, costing twenty-four killed, forty injured and £44,795 damage, caused widespread concern in the city and resulted in riots during which many shopkeepers with German-sounding names had their property attacked.

The consolation to this raid was the destruction of Army airship LZ 37 by Flt-Sub-Lt Warnford of No 1 Squadron RNAS over Ghent as it approached its base in Belgium. LZ 38 was bombed in its Evere hangar shortly after docking on its return. Another short lived consolation for the residents of Hull was the installation of a gun on the roof of a factory. It was soon found to be made of wood!

Total devastation at Edwin Place off Porter Street following the German air raid of 6 June 1915. Three people died here. Porter Street has now been totally redeveloped and is the site of several multi-story tower blocks of flats.

This is probably East Street off Church Street after a visit by Zeppelin L 9 on the night of 5-6 June 1915. Church Street, not far from Drypool Bridge, is now almost wholly occupied by industrial estates. In 1915 three people died here and 'several' were injured.

The Naval Wing of the Royal Flying Corps (RNAS) had opened an aerodrome at Gosforth, Newcastle, in November 1914 to be followed by the requisitioning of land to provide landing facilities at Whitley Bay (February 1915), Redcar (July 1915) and Scarborough racecourse, also in July, to support its Home Defence responsibilities. A landing ground at Atwick to the north of Hornsea was also requisitioned at the same time. Redcar was developed into an aerodrome but Atwick remained a landing ground with limited services until Special Duties squadrons were formed using the Airco DH6 which required additional facilities.

Scarborough and Atwick were used from the early August of 1915. Shortly after arrival at Atwick the RNAS were called to action on the evening of 9 August when Navy Zeppelin L 9 (*Kptlt* Odo Loewe) appeared off Flamborough Head at 20.15 and nosed over the coast twice. The RNAS had already had warning of the intruder and had flown several patrols from Redcar and Scarborough and an AZP (Anti-Zeppelin Patrol) was flown from Atwick.

The night raids continued through 1915 and by the end of that year the Germans had made twenty raids by some forty-four airships dropping an estimated 196 tons of bombs. These killed 193, injured 528 civilians and caused £807,818 material damage. On the other side of the coin the RFC and RNAS flew 115 sorties and destroyed two airships, one on its home base by No 1 Squadron RNAS, based

Numbers 1, 2 and 3 St Thomas's Terrace off Campbell Street on 7 June 1915. The gap in the centre is what remains of number 2 and is where four members of the Walker family were killed. Constable Hatfield of the North-Eastern Railway Police lived with his wife and four children at number 3, but despite the damage all escaped unharmed. Campbell Street ran north off the old Hessle Road, originating where the flyover now runs. The whole area suffered even more in the Second World War and has now been completely redeveloped.

This is probably the kitchen/scullery of 21 or 22 Edwin Place off Porter Street after 6 June 1915, showing it to be completely burnt out. Three people died here.

A view looking along St Thomas's Terrace, presumably so named on account of the church opposite. In one of the most gruesome incidents of the entire Zeppelin raid of 6 June, the body of the unfortunate Alice Walker, still on her bed, was blown onto the aisle roof.

Two views of the devastated sawmill fronting Dansom Lane which was burnt out by enemy bombs on the night of June 6 1915. The upper view is almost certainly taken looking north-east along Bright Street opposite where number 30 was also destroyed that night. The large building in the background in the lower view is where Reckitt & Colman still remains (now as Reckitt Benckiser), on the opposite side of Dansom Lane to the saw mill. The editor of this book grew up in Beeton Street, less than 200 yards from here.

in France, and one damaged by ground fire. The defence fighter force lost three aircrew killed and fifteen aircraft damaged

By late 1915 it was obvious that the defence against the night intruders was somewhat lacking, indeed many members of the armed forces thought that there was no defence. Detection and interception control was rudimentary and night flying navigation was in its infancy. The War Office and the Admiralty could not agree on their respective responsibilities for the lines and areas of home defence. It was argued that the navy deal with enemy aircraft approaching the coast and the army take over when they had crossed the coast – about the only things they could agree on were that Zeppelins were difficult to find in the dark and night flying was fraught with problems. Eventually the War Cabinet told the War Office to raise Home Defence (HD) Squadrons which were to be administered by the Home Wing Brigade.

These HD squadrons were in general located on the eastern side of mainland Britain and in particular were positioned to provide the best defence for London, the industrial areas of the Midlands and the north of England. A squadron normally comprised a Headquarters and 'A', 'B' and 'C' Flights. The HQ was often located at a central location to the Flight Station aerodromes. In addition to the requirement to provide aerodromes

having servicing facilities and personnel accommodation, landing grounds were also established in the squadron areas to cater for emergencies. These landing grounds were in the main intended for night use and were pieces of requisitioned farmland that could be cleared of livestock and agricultural obstructions when operations were expected. Each had a rudimentary shelter for ground staff and storage for runway marker flares. Each HD squadron was given the control of a searchlight company.

At the beginning of 1917 there were eleven dedicated HD squadrons, each operating three flights based on fully equipped aerodromes with the headquarters located at some central site. In addition some 140 landing grounds, all graded as to condition, were available. The RNAS also established aerodromes and landing grounds from which its Home Defence responsibilities could be discharged.

Aerodrome and landing ground flarepaths prior to 1916 were created with cans containing petrol soaked cotton waste, which proved to be expensive in petrol. By March 1917 the Money Flare became the standard. In this case the flare comprised a wire basket containing asbestos wool which was soaked by dipping in a bucket of paraffin. The flare used about ten pints of paraffin an hour, required little maintenance and could penetrate mist and fog. The Money Flare was not bettered

This was the scene at St Thomas's Terrace off Campbell Street (close to where the Hessle Road flyover now runs) shortly after the first air raid on Hull on 6 June 1915. Four people were killed here and three injured. A macabre detail is the light spot on the roof of the small lean-to on the right, which is an undamaged chamber pot.

throughout the war and was supplemented by the Lyons searchlight and small acetylene lamps when the aeroplane had landed. All obstructions on the approach to aerodromes and landing grounds were initially required to be lit by red lights. This was found to be confusing and by March 1917 only the first obstruction on the approach to the flarepath and the first on take-off were lit. All other directions were deemed to be dangerous. Aerial lighthouses flashing recognition letters were introduced in 1917 at aerodromes and on patrol boundaries. With the introduction of

used a microphone instead of the sound trumpet. The bearings of the noise source were passed to the HD organisation. Examples of the Sound Mirrors still exist on the east coast at Kilnsea, Boulby, Redcar and Sunderland.

The Home Wing Brigade, after many changes in designation became the 6th (HD) Brigade in October 1917.

The most numerous aeroplane in the Royal Flying Corps Home Defence squadron establishment was initially the BE2c, a two-seat tractor biplane powered by a Royal Aircraft Factory 70hp air-cooled in-line engine.

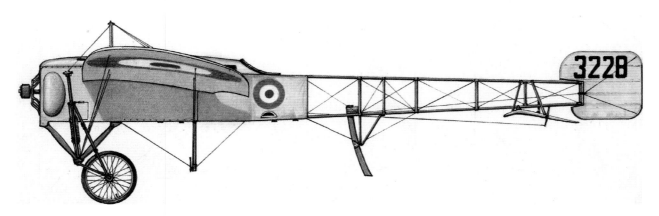

Blériot XI-2 3228 of 'D' Flight RNAS Hornsea and flown by Flt Sub-Lt R G Mack on the evening of 9/10 August 1915 in a vain attempt to intercept the Zeppelin L 9 (commanded by Kptlt Loewe) which passed directly over Atwick, with the intention of attacking Hull. In fact the ground mist confused him to such an extent that he bombed Goole in error. There the forty-two bombs dropped killed sixteen people and wounded eleven. Despite the best efforts of the RNAS pilot, such an elderly machine was unable to achieve much and Mack crashed in dense fog while trying to land at Atwick. The aircraft was subsequently written off. Its finish is typical of the period: clear-doped linen fabric and all other materials in their natural finish.

R/T (radio telephony) in 1918, 80ft high masts were erected adjacent to the hangars and illuminated with green lights. The responsibility for maintaining the lighting at landing grounds was initially with the Volunteer Detachments but this was taken over by detachments of the Royal Defence Corps, which in mid-1917 had been formed into the 19th Bn RDC. After April 1918 the 19th Bn became the General Duties Unit, RAF, with a strength of 17 officers and 1162 other ranks in November 1918.

The detection of incoming enemy raiders created considerable thought and research, and development led to the installation of Sound Mirrors along the eastern English Channel and North Sea coasts. These took the form of a concave concrete bowl of 15ft diameter, in some examples with projecting wings at the side which reduced interference. A rotatable sound trumpet was positioned centrally some distance in front of the bowl to maximise the collected sound and angular azimuth readings could be made of the sound bearing. Later versions of the Sound Mirrors

Developed by the Royal Aircraft Factory at Farnborough and, in common with many aeroplanes of that period, production was sub-contracted to many manufacturers. The inherent stability of the BE2c which made it unsuitable for air to air fighting was to its advantage for night flying and making night landings. Although normally a two-seater most of the Home Defence machines were flown solo with the front cockpit faired over. The offensive armament was one fixed Vickers machine gun mounted to the front of the pilot, to fire upwards from behind the top wing, and may include four 20lb HE or 16lb incendiary bombs, a box of 24 Ranken Darts and four or five drums of ammunition. The bombs and 1lb explosive darts were intended to be dropped from above to pierce the Zeppelin envelope in the hope that the gas would escape and then be ignited by the sparks from the black powder in the exploding dart or by incendiary bullets. As the BE2c took an hour to reach 10,000ft, the usual operational height of the Zeppelin, this method of attack seldom achieved results.

Defence policy at the time was to have two

aeroplanes at readiness and one on standby. The procedure was for one to take off as soon as a warning was received and patrol the squadron patrol area at 8-10,000ft for two hours. This required adequate warning time to allow for climb to patrol height; the second aeroplane was to follow ninety minutes later. A system of signals on the ground was developed to indicate the latest known direction of the intruder. Often the readiness aeroplanes would be detached to an adjacent landing ground.

In addition to its Home Defence commitment the RNAS still had the responsibility for coastal waters patrols. Consequently it had opened a sub-station to Killingholme at Hornsea Mere. Appreciating the need to extend the patrol cover of |the airship throughout British coastal waters the Admiralty established an airship station at Howden. This opened in June of 1916 and a mooring out station to Howden was opened at Lowthorpe in 1918.

By 1917 the Zeppelin threat was considered to be lower and as a result the number of aeroplanes required for the Home Defence commitment of the UK based squadrons was scaled down. Additionally the attrition rate of pilots on the Western Front was growing to such an extent that an increase in pilot training was seen to be required.

With the outbreak of war in August 1914 the three original RFC Squadrons had been expanded to seven and it was becoming apparent that further expansion would be required. To accommodate this expansion it was apparent that the increase in the number of trained pilots required to man these extra squadrons would be beyond the training resources of the Central Flying School at Upavon. Prior to 1914 the training of pilots was carried out at civil flying schools and from August 1912 military aviators were trained at the Central Flying School at Upavon. To cater for this training need No 1 Reserve Aeroplane Squadron was formed at Farnborough in August 1914. The number of Reserve Aeroplane Schools was increased to meet the demand for pilots and they were renamed Reserve Squadrons on 13 January 1916. Training standards were constantly under review and in March 1916 Qualification Tests were drawn up as follows:

1) The Pilot must have spent at least 15 hours in the air solo.

2) He must have flown a service aeroplane satisfactorily.

3) He must have carried out a cross country flight of at least 60 miles successfully. During this flight he must land at two outside landing places under the supervision of an officer of the RFC.

4) He will climb to 6,000 ft and remain at that height for at least 15 minutes, after which he will land with his engine stopped, the aeroplane first touching the ground within a circular mark of 50yds diameter. This test can be combined with (3) if proper supervision can be arranged.

5) He will make two landings in the dark assisted by flares.

During late 1916 it was decided to categorise the Reserve Squadrons into Elementary and Higher types, students moving from one to another before posting to a service squadron. This reduced the training commitment on units working up to operational status. The test requirements for graduate pilots were constantly under review and by 1918 had been revised for the various categories of front line pilots, i.e. fighter, bomber etc, being trained for duty in the newly-formed Royal Air Force.

On 3 August 1918 6th Brigade issued orders for the training of pilots with a summary of the tests for categories A, B, and C that were applicable to Day and Night Fighting Pilots, Northern Defence Pilots and Light Night Bombing Pilots. The three categories were:

CATEGORY A

(Applicable to Day and Night Fighting, Northern Defence, and Light Night Bombing Pilots).

1 Examination A at School of Military Aeronautics.

2 All Day and Night Ground Gunnery Tests.

3 All Elementary Aerial Navigation Tests.

4 Pupils to have completed 15 hours solo and have received instruction as laid down in Flying Instructions Chapter III to end of Chapter 10.

Incident
On the night of 21 August 1917 a contentious Zeppelin raid took place over the East Riding and Hull. Officially denied by British authorities at the time, it is now clear that at least three out of a fleet of eight Zeppelins made landfall in the area and dropped their bombs. L 41 (Hptmn Manger) was driven off by gunfire from Hull, instead dropping his bombs on Paull, Preston, Thorngumbald and Hedon. Only Hedon suffered damage, which included the destruction of a Methodist chapel and damage to other properties. One man was injured. L 42 (Dietrich) attacked ships off Spurn Head, while L 45 (Kölle) bombed British warships off Withernsea. Although damage was minimal, it was found that by operating at an altitude of 20,000ft, the Zeppelins were almost immune to gunfire and air attack.
Zeppelins passed near Hull on 20 October 1917 when L 41 (Manger) and L 45 (Kölle) made landfall near the Humber. L 45 circled around near Withernsea for an hour, but their attacks were directed against the Midlands.
The last Zeppelin raid on the East Riding occurred on 12 March 1918 when L 63 (Kptlt von Freudenreich) made landfall over Hornsea and followed the railway line to Hull. There he scattered bombs around Sutton and Swine and six within Hull. One woman 'died of shock'. Meanwhile L 62 (Manger) attempted unsuccessfully to attack the RNAS airship station at Howden. The final visit by a Zeppelin to the area was when L 61 (Kptlt Ehrlich) passed over Withernsea on 13 August 1918 en-route to attack Wigan. For East Yorkshire the day of the Zeppelin was over.

CATEGORY B

5   *25 hours solo since commencing instruction. 4 hours night flying. Flown a Service Aeroplane successfully.*

6   *All Wireless Tests.*

7   *All Advanced Aerial Navigation Tests.*

8   *Flight to 10000ft and descent with engine shut off, landing within 50yds of a mark.*

9   *60 miles Day Cross Country Flight.*

10   *(Day and Night Fighting Pilots) Cross Country Flight in Dark Goggles. (Northern Defence Pilots) 60 miles Night Reconnaissance.*

CATEGORY C

Day and Night Fighting Pilots

1   *Advanced Gunnery Tests.*

2   *Day Aerial Fighting.*

3   *Formation Flying.*

4   *Skilled Pilot on Service Machine and Night.*

5   *Ceiling Test repeated monthly, 19000ft on Sopwith Camel or Bristol Fighter.*

6   *Qualified to ascend on Day Raids by Hostile Aircraft.*

Northern Defence Pilots

1   *Advanced Gunnery Tests.*

2   *Day Aerial Fighting.*

3   *Dummy bomb dropping by Day.*

4   *100 mile Night Reconnaissance*

5   *Ceiling Test repeated monthly, 17,000ft on 110hp Le Rhone Avro.*

6   *Qualified to ascend on Night Raids by Hostile Aircraft.*

The training establishments went through several changes of title, ie Training Squadron, Training Depot Station, although the training function did not change with the alteration of name. The two training aerodromes in the East Riding, Beverley and Driffeld, were training single-seat fighter pilots. Light Night Bombing Pilots were trained at specialist units.

The requirement for increasing the training rate of pilots and observers was not the only problem the infant air force had. By 1916/7 there was a growing shortage of men to service and repair the machines of the RFC. The military recruiting system paid scant regard to the civilian job of the volunteer or conscript; as a result very many men were put into the trenches who had the mechanical and wood working skills needed. Consequently the training of ground tradesmen was started and training schools were opened. In addition the recruitment of women was started in 1917 for the Women's Companies in the RFC. As in the civilian factories these service women carried out a variety of duties. These units became the Women's Royal Air Force (not to be confused with the WAAF of the Second World War and the later WRAF) in 1918. Women were also employed on the UK aerodromes for domestic duties and were referred to as Hostel Staff.

Fields and Sheds

Aerodrome buildings of the First World War

2

While the opening dates of the local aerodromes are documented, as are the arrival of the user elements, this does not mean that the aerodrome sites were complete at opening date. The survey carried out in August 1918 by the newly-formed Royal Air Force reveals that in most cases the major buildings of the establishments were nearly complete, but there was still work to do and completion was not expected until later that year, which would indicate a construction phase of some two years. In common with the aerodromes of the 1939-1945 war, the largest buildings on the site were the hangars or 'Aeroplane Sheds' as they were known at that period, a title that continued in use into the expansion period of the mid-thirties. Several designs of aeroplane sheds were used during the First World War.

The earliest design to be erected on the Home Defence and Training aerodromes in 1915-16 was the 1913-pattern 'Side Entry Shed', 160 ft in length, with a span of 65ft. The roof was ridged along the length with a ridged gable at right angles midway along the length. Entry was, as the name suggests, at the side below the gable with a free opening of 58ft 6in and a clear height of 15ft, which was closed by sliding doors. Many aerodromes had twin or coupled Side Entry Sheds which had a length of 211ft and with entries below the two gables. The two gables at right angles to the roof ridge gave a very distinctive roof outline in plan. Construction varied from wooden frames and roof trusses to steel frame and roof trusses. Sides and roofs were of timber and felt, corrugated steel or asbestos sheeting, while some survivors have been brick-clad. Ventilation louvres were provided along the roof line. Offices, stores, dressing-rooms and workshops were provided in an annexe built along the rear wall. Examples of the Coupled

Coupled 80ft span General Service Sheds at Old Sarum, near Salisbury. These sheds are of a later pattern with brick side walls and arched brick door supports replacing the timber construction.

Side Entry shed may be found today at Montrose, Netheravon and Catterick. The latter have had the side walls brick-clad.

Initially many of the Home Defence squadron aerodromes had the Aeroplane Twin Shed, also known as the HD Aeroplane Shed. Of all timber construction with the timber roof trusses supported on externally braced wall-posts, the centre of the trusses resting on timber support piers and the spaces between the central piers were left open. The roof and external walls were timber planked and one end was open and closed by canvas curtains, while the other was closed with planking and fitted with large ventilation louvres. Later sheds had sliding doors. These double sheds had distinctive double pitched roofs and measured 130ft by 120ft. Photographs of the period reveal that on some aerodromes, quite often overseas, single versions of the shed are apparent. A site plan of the aerodrome at St Omer in France drawn by the Royal Engineers in 1918 shows 13 Type 'B' Hangars, of which four are shown as singles. From illustrations and photographs the Type 'B'

corresponds to the Aeroplane Twin Shed and its single variant. Twin Aeroplane Sheds may have been erected on some aerodromes in the East Riding and later demolished to be replaced by the General Service Shed, but there is no evidence that this was so.

Introduced from 1916, the General Service Shed became the standard on most United Kingdom aerodromes constructed through to 1918. The roof trusses, known as the Belfast truss after the original developers in the town of the same name, gave the GS sheds a distinctive bowed outline to the roof in end elevation. GS sheds are now often known as 'Belfast hangars'. The roof trusses were supported at the outer end on timber posts and braced, in early examples, with timber 'A' frames. In later examples the timber side bracing frames were replaced by metal frames. The roof trusses were supplied in two span sizes: 80ft and 100ft. In general the roof trusses were spaced in 11ft 6in bays giving a total shed length of 172ft 6in. Annexes were attached to the outer walls. The end openings

A twin or coupled 1913 Pattern Side Entry Shed. This particular shed is on the First and Second World War aerodrome at Montrose where two examples are preserved.

An example of the Twin Aeroplane Shed or Type 'B' Hangar at an unknown location. It is possible, but thought unlikely, that a few such sheds were initially erected for use by Home Defence squadrons in East Yorkshire.

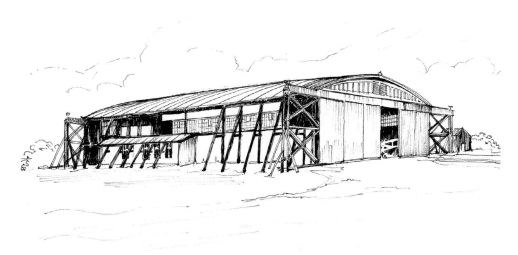

This sketch shows an early General Service Shed of the 1916 period with the timber structure to support the open doors.

Belfast Trusses in the roof of the Bramham Moor General Service Shed. The roof of the building has listed protection.

An example of a single 100ft span General Service Shed at Harling Road, Norfolk. This shed was originally used as the Aircraft Repair Shed and, as with other sheds that were on the site, was of brick construction with an annexe to the airfield side.

The external timber bracing for the roof trusses and wall piers of the Bramham Moor General Service Shed.

of 80 or 100ft had a clear open height of 20 or 25ft and were closed by sliding doors running in metal tracks, the lower tracks set in concrete. The upper tracks were supported at the outer ends by a wooden gantry construction or in the case of later buildings by arched brick piers. The roof was covered with timber and felt cladding, the side walls were timber with bituminous felt cladding. General Service Sheds built later during the war were in the main of brick construction. The roof trusses were still made in timber but were supported on brick piers which were externally braced by brick buttresses. The space between the external piers was in-filled with brick and the glazing in each bay covered half the height. Many GS sheds were built as twin or coupled units having internal widths of 120 or 200ft. The central supports for the trusses were brick or timber piers, the spaces between the central piers were not in-filled. When open, the sliding doors were also supported in brick-built arched supports. The sheds erected at the end of the war had the Esavian Type 120 concertina-folding teak doors which folded back into brick 'L' shaped end supports. Listed examples of the 'Belfast' GS aeroplane shed can be found today at many sites in the United Kingdom, the nearest example to the East Riding being an early

The last General Service Sheds to be constructed retained the 'Belfast' bowed roof outline and the side walls were of brick construction. By 1918 the sliding doors to the 100ft span Shed were being replaced by the Esavian concertina folding teak doors, as these examples at the Imperial War Museum, Duxford, which opened to 'L' shaped door stops.

example of a single GS shed at the Leeds University farm, Headley Hall, to the south west of Tadcaster (on what was Bramham Moor aerodrome in the First World War). This building has external timber 'A' frame roof truss supports and would have had the wooden door support gantries but these are now long gone. The lower metal door runner rails set in concrete still exist.

Another aircraft shelter in general use during the war was the Bessoneau Hangar. Of French design, hence the name: 'hangar' is the French for aeroplane shelter. The Bessoneau was a truly portable device constructed from timber 'A' frames supporting timber roof trusses and covered with heavy canvas. Entry was at one end only, which was closed by canvas curtains. The standard Bessoneau in general use by the Naval and Military Wings of the RFC had a span of about 65ft and came in two lengths, 80 and 118ft. The hangar could be erected by twenty skilled men in forty-eight hours.

The Field Service Pocket Book of April 1918 states that the standard Bessoneau in RAF use could be transported in five lorries (one with hoops taken off) for a short journey, a longer journey required six lorries, or four with trailers. For movement by rail two railway trucks, not less than 33ft long were needed. The Bessoneau Hangar remained in the RAF stores inventory as standard issue until the late thirties and some were still in existence well after the Second World War.

Generally the buildings on the aerodromes were grouped into two categories, 'Technical' and 'Regimental', designating their use. The Technical Site comprised aeroplane sheds, workshops, classrooms and offices which were usually co-located. Workshops at some sites were possibly of temporary brick or concrete construction with timber roof trusses and timber and felt or corrugated asbestos roof covering. In size they appear to have been 100 to 130ft long by 28ft. Other buildings were to

Most of the existing examples of the early General Service Sheds have had the wooden door supports removed as with this surviving example at the First World War aerodrome site on Bramham Moor, Tadcaster.

Another view of a single 100ft span General Service Shed at Harling Road, Norfolk.

the standard 28ft width but their length was generally in the order of 30ft. As far as can be ascertained, the offices and other buildings, with the exception of explosives or flammable stores, were of standard sectional timber units. The Regimental Site, usually detached from the Technical Site, was the domestic area and contained barrack blocks, messes, institution, ablutions and Guard Room/reception etc. The officers' facilities were usually separated from the Other Ranks and the women's hostel was sited apart from those buildings for male use. The Regimental buildings were, generally, wooden huts, standing on brick plinths, and linked to give the desired format using standard sectional units. Similar sectional wooden huts are still in use at many aerodromes and some may even date back to the First World War.

Machine gun butts, firing ranges and explosive stores were located well away from the buildings, as was the circle marked out on the grass field that was used as the aiming mark for practice bombing. An item on an aerodrome that may have survived at many sites is the Compass Platform. A circular concrete pad, the diameter depending on the aeroplane size at the station, this was the location where the accuracy of the aeroplane compass when installed in the airframe was checked for deviation in heading. This was, and still is, achieved by turning the aircraft through 360 degrees and checking for deviation of the displayed heading against an external master compass.

These workshop buildings at Beverley Racecourse on the Westwood are reputed to date from the First World War aerodrome period.

The Aerodromes

3

Beverley

In 1915 the military authorities advised Beverley Town Council that they intended to requisition 179 acres of the Westwood, including the race course and some of the adjoining land to the north of the Hurn, on which to establish an aerodrome. The Town Council was requested to make the necessary arrangements for drainage and other details connected with the aerodrome. An Aerodrome Committee was therefore formed within the Council. From reading the subsequent Town Council minutes it appears that their only interest in the project was the rate to be charged for water supply and sewage disposal into the Town's system — the old Yorkshire adage 'where there's muck there's money' springs to mind!

Consequently, the existing racecourse was taken over, apart from an area between the eastern extremity of the course and the houses adjacent to the Hurn. A further 50

acres to the north and west of the racecourse boundary was also taken. From an aerial photograph dated 1917, it would appear that the flying area was located on this land. The terrain to the south and east, ie that contained within the racecourse, was not suitable for aircraft operations. The aerodrome buildings were located just to the west of today's racecourse buildings.

With the formation of No 47 Squadron on 1 March 1916, under the command of Capt P G Small, the aerodrome was formally opened. The Squadron was given temporary Home Defence responsibilities within the structure of the 6th Brigade of the RFC, which had overall responsibility for UK Home Defence against air attack.

At this time the type of buildings on the aerodrome is not known but there are reports of tents in the area and reference to photographs dating to No 47 Squadron's

This operational Wolseley-built BE2c, 2650, is typical of the aircraft allocated to the early Home Defence squadrons in East Yorkshire. Little is known about the military service of 'Tasman' or where this picture was taken, but B.E.2c 2661 served with 33 (HD) Squadron at Beverley. With a degree of luck the BE2c could make an effective anti-Zeppelin weapon; certainly Lt William Leefe Robinson used 2693 to shoot down SL 11 on 2/3 September 1916.

An aerial view of the RFC station on Beverley Westwood, taken on 7 May 1917 by an aircraft from No. 36 (Training) Squadron.

occupancy show the existence of at least one 1913 pattern Coupled Side Entry Shed.

Security requirements closed the main road to York and sentries were placed at its junction with the Newbald Road on the east and to the west at the Killingwoldgraves cross roads. Passes were issued to those who had to travel into Beverley for work but this did not stop the local youngsters approaching the aerodrome across the Westwood.

Four days after the formation of No 47 Squadron, on the night of 5/6 March 1916, three German Navy Zeppelins, L 11, L 13, and L 14, left their base to attack British naval installations at Rosyth and the Tyne/Tees area.

The unforecast weather with 50 mph north-westerly winds and heavy snow showers caused the three Zeppelin commanders to abandon the planned attacks by 1700 hrs and to look for targets further to the south. L 14, under the command of *Kptlt* Aloys Böcker, crossed the Yorkshire coast at Flamborough Head at 2230 hrs and headed south dropping six bombs at Beverley. This air raid on Beverley is reported in the Minutes of a Beverley Town Council meeting held on the following day, but apart from saying that the bombs were dropped in the vicinity of the Gas Works in Figham Road and that a sub-committee was formed to report on the incident, the precise impact points of the bombs is not recorded. A Council meeting held a month later minutes that the sub-committee report was submitted and lists the actions to be taken in the event of other air raids. There is no record today of the actual report in the East Riding Archives at Beverley.

After bombing Beverley L 14 eventually located the Humber and around midnight bombed Hull, releasing seven explosive and thirteen incendiary bombs, which fell mainly on houses in the vicinity of the docks. Böcker decided against making a second bombing run because of the winds and departed Hull for his home base at 0100 hrs. Ten minutes after the departure of L 14, Zeppelin L 11 in command of *Kvtkpt* Viktor Schütze, arrived over Hull. He had crossed the coast near Withernsea earlier at 2145 hrs, and then roamed around East Yorkshire and North Lincolnshire, lost in the heavy snowstorms. Through a clearance in the weather Schütze identified Hull and saw the explosions from the bombs dropped by L 14. At 0110 hrs Schütze descended to 4,500ft and stayed over the city for twenty minutes releasing one and a half tons of bombs, damaging houses in the old town area. The two raids over the night of 5/6 March caused eighteen deaths and injury to over fifty persons and £25,000 damage. On its way home L 11 dropped bombs at Killingholme on the south bank of the Humber. The third Zeppelin, L 13, (*Kptlt* H Mathy) had an engine failure over the North Sea but made good time to cross the Humber at 2145 hrs. The strong winds and snowstorms made navigation extremely difficult and after reaching Newark Mathy turned to the south-east and eventually found himself over the Thames estuary, 150 miles to the south of his estimated position. He finally exited the English airspace at 0202 hrs.

While all this enemy air activity was taking place, the recently-formed No 47 Squadron was not ready for action, and in fact the atrocious weather conditions precluded home defence operations by any Northern squadron. Only one sortie was made on that night, by a BE2c from RNAS Eastchurch.

In January of 1916 No 33 Squadron had been formed at Filton as part of the Home Defence force, moving to the North on 29 March in the same year. Their headquarters, under Maj P B Joubert de la Ferte, were located at Bramham Moor (Tadcaster) with flights

MINUTES of the Proceedings of the COUNCIL in COMMITTEE, at the Guildhall, the 3rd April, 1916.

Present—

The Mayor, Chairman.

Aldermen CARE, ELWELL, SCHOFIELD, WESTERBY, WOOD.

Councillors ARDEN, BUTT, CHERRY, FOLEY, FOX, GATES, HAMMOND, HOBSON, D. NUTCHEY, PEPPER, VERNON.

The Town Clerk.

1 The Committee considered a report of the Sub-Committee appointed by the Town Council to investigate the facts in connection with the dropping of bombs by hostile aircraft in the vicinity of the Gasworks on the night of the 5th/6th March, 1916, together with recommendations as to the steps to be taken for the safety of the public in the event of future alarms.

RESOLVED that the Report be received and adopted, and that the recommendations therein contained be approved as follows :—

(i) That on receipt of information from the Acting Chief Constable, or other competent authority, that the preliminary warning of the approach of air craft has been received, the Gas Manager shall attend forthwith at the Chief Constable's Office to receive instructions as to the steps to be taken for dealing with the public and private lights, and shall then take up his station at the Gasworks and remain there until he is released by the Acting Chief Constable.

detached to Coal Aston (A Flight), and Beverley (C Flight) with temporary detachments to Doncaster and The Knavesmire in York. Two flights from 47 Squadron were detached at Beverley to No 33 Squadron.

The units at Beverley were soon, however, involved in defensive operations. On the night of 1/2 April 1916 Navy Zeppelins L 11 (*Kvtkpt* V. Schütze) and L 17 (*Kptlt* H. Ehrlich) targeted northern England. Among the seven sorties flown by the RNAS and the RFC, one BE2c of 47 Squadron was airborne but crashed following engine failure. Although not stationed in the East Riding, an Avro 504C piloted by Sub-Lt Roche from RNAS Scarborough force-landed on the cliffs at Speeton. On the night of 5/6 April L 11, L 16 and L 13 set out to attack northern England again. Navy Zeppelin L 11 (*Kvtkpt* V. Schutze) crossed the coast at Hornsea at 2105 hrs. On approaching Hull at 2120 hrs it was met with heavy anti-aircraft fire and after dropping four bombs retreated out to sea. No 47 Squadron put up two BE2c aeroplanes, one of which was piloted by Capt P G Small and the other, 2720, was flown by Lt N Bottomley. After a vain search

Extract from the Minutes of a Beverley Town Council Meeting held on 3 April 1915.

for L 11, Bottomley experienced an exciting landing back at Beverley when the throttle would not fully close and his machine was badly damaged, but he was unhurt. Lt Bottomley, with the repaired 2720, was again involved on the night of 2/3 May with Lt D C Rutter, in BE2c 2721, but driving rain and heavy cloud prevented take-off until 03.00 on the 3rd, by which time the threat against local targets had diminished. A patrol was flown, however, off the Humber and the coast but the weather made navigation difficult and the two aeroplanes landed back at Beverley after a forty-five minute patrol.

One of the naval Zeppelins, L 21, (*Kptlt* Max Dietrich), crossed the English coast north of Scarborough at 2140 hrs and at 2240 hrs attacked York for ten minutes. L 21 then departed near Bridlington. Defence sorties were flown by RFC units in North Yorkshire and the RNAS at Scarborough, Redcar and Whitley Bay. No 47 Squadron had two BE2cs at readiness in case an attack on Hull developed, each readiness aircraft armed with four 16lb HE bombs, six incendiaries and a box of Ranken darts. Heavy rain and cloud lasted most of the night, however, and prevented

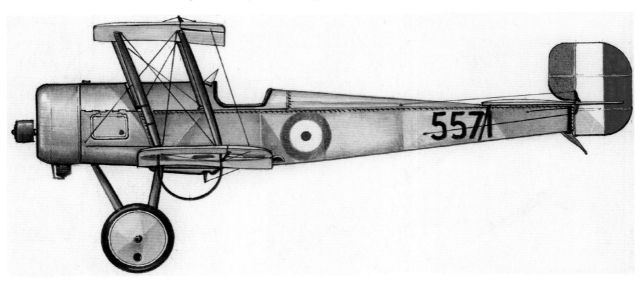

Finished in similar fashion to the Blériot on page 20, this Bristol 'Scout' Type D, 5571, served at Beverley with No 47 Squadron between June-July 1916 and No 33 (HD) Squadron before finally ending its service days with No 55 (Reserve) Squadron at Yatesbury.

At this stage of the war the Home Defence squadrons had, in addition to their defence responsibilities, the task of training the graduate pilots posted to them following basic training. It was then the responsibility of the senior pilots of the squadron to bring them up to a level where they were considered to be competent. As a result the HD squadrons had a mix of aeroplanes on their establishment. No 47 Squadron operated BE2c, AW FK3, Bristol Scout and BE12 aircraft. No 33 Squadron were involved for a longer period on home defence duties and had on their strength until 1919 Avro 504s, several marks of the BE2 and BE12, RAF FE2b and 2d, Bristol F2B and a night fighter version of the Avro 504K.

On the night of 2/3 May an attacking force of nine Zeppelins set out to target Rosyth, the Forth Bridge (navy) and Manchester (army), but adverse weather with strong winds forced the navy Zeppelins to head for the Midlands.

take-off. BE2c 2720, with Lt N H Bottomley and BE2c (2721) flown by Lt D C Rutter, took off at 0305 hrs and 0300 hrs respectively and patrolled the Humber and nearby coast looking for stragglers. Heavy cloud made navigation difficult and both pilots returned to Beverley after a forty-five minute patrol.

No Zeppelin attacks were made against England during the long summer nights of June 1916 and No 47 Squadron was withdrawn from Home Defence commitments in September, re-equipped with Bristol Scouts and posted to Salonika. The summer nights that caused a temporary halt to the Zeppelin attacks also coincided with a reduction in coastal attacks by aeroplanes; this strengthened authority thinking that greater priority should be given to the Western Front and the planned Home Defence force of ten squadrons was cut to eight. No 33 Squadron remained in being, although the exigencies of the attrition rate on the

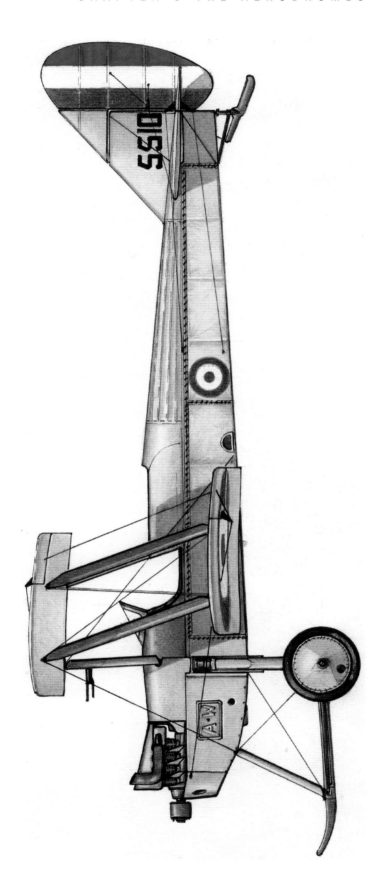

*An Armstrong-Whitworth
FK3 in typically nondescript
and simple finish serving
with 47 Squadron at
Beverley in spring 1916.*

Above: *Seen at Yatesbury, and illustrated in colour on page 32, Bristol Scout D, 5571 saw service with No. 33 (HD) Squadron at Beverley in April 1916.*

Right: *Avro 504K E3033 in night-fighter finish served with 33 Squadron and is seen here at Kirton-in-Lindsey late in the war.*

On the strength of No 47 Squadron between June and July 1916 was Bristol Scout D, 5570. Unusually for a Scout, it is finished in khaki PC10 or PC12 dope. This accident was at Yatesbury after 47 Squadron had gone to the Middle East. Clearly the damage was repairable as post-war 5570 became civilianised as G-EAGR.

This Avro 504A, D6272, photographed inverted was built by The Humber Motor Company at Coventry. It served with No 72 Squadron while at Beverley. The Avro 504 in its various models was a standard training machine throughout the RFC and RAF.

Left: This Armstrong Whitworth FK3, 5512, photographed outside one of the twin Side Entry sheds at RFC Beverley, was on the establishment of No 47 Squadron. It is finished in the usual clear dope of the early RFC aircraft.

Below: Armstrong Whitworth FK3, 6191, was on the strength of No 47 Squadron between March and September 1916 and may have been photographed at RFC station Beverley after an early spring snowfall. Note its well-worn appearance.

Western Front resulted in the strength of the Squadron being reduced to six aircraft instead of a planned establishment of 18.

In 1916 much of the operational flying by the HD squadrons was at night and a series of night landing grounds were established, mainly for possible emergency use, but in some cases to locate a detachment of two duty aircraft and pilots closer to the possible flight path of the enemy. These landing grounds, basically meadows of minimal dimensions, needed to be relatively level, have no obstructions and reasonably short grass. They were manned by a few personnel and equipped with some aviation fuel and flares to mark the landing area. Accommodation was a tent or hut and a telephone. In some cases the local farmer would be asked to remove his cows as the field was to be used for a detachment. In general the landing grounds were known by the name of the nearest railway station. No 33 Squadron had landing grounds at South Cave, Hedon, Bellasize,

Atwick and Owthorne. In the case of the latter two the facilities were shared with the RNAS.

Capt R C L Holme of No 33 Squadron flew a patrol from 0225 hrs to 0335 hrs on the night of 2/3 August in response to an attack by L 11, L 13, L 16, L 17, L 21, and L 31 against the East Anglia coast. Although an alert was still in force during his patrol the raiders had departed.

A month later the Germans launched the biggest Zeppelin attack of the war against London with Navy Zeppelins L 11, L 13, L 14, L 16, L 21, L 22, L 23, L 24, L 30, L 32, Navy Schutte-Lanz SL 18, Army Zeppelins LZ 90, LZ 97, LZ 98 and Army Schutte-Lanz SL 11. Adverse winds, belts of heavy rain and icing at high altitude caused the enemy force to be widely dispersed with only one airship penetrating to within seven miles of the centre of London. Sixteen to seventeen tons of bombs were scattered from the Humber to Gravesend resulting in four killed, twelve injured and £21,072 worth of damage on the ground. The

An unidentified group, probably taken shortly after the formation of the RAF. The officer with the cane appears to wear naval uniform in khaki. Standing behind him is an army private, while the other men all wear RFC uniform and that Service's 'maternity' jacket. The ladies are members of the WRAF. Visible shoulder flashes all read 'Royal Flying Corps'.

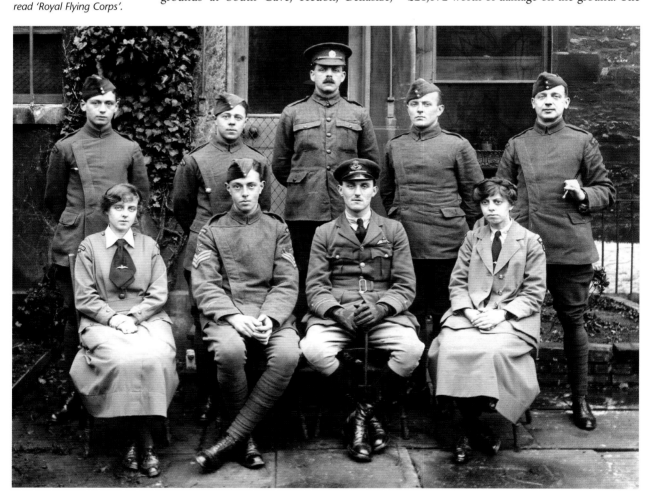

HD squadrons mounted sixteen defence sorties in response to these intrusions. L 22 (*Kptlt* Martin Dietrich) passed about ten miles to the south of Beverley after dropping a few bombs on Humberston, near Grimsby, and 'C' Flight of No 33 Squadron at Beverley mounted one of these sorties in an attempt to intercept. Unfortunately, this sortie by Capt R C L Holme in BE2c 2661 ended at 0025 hrs when he crashed on take-off. Capt Holme was unhurt.

The final defence sortie by No 33 Squadron from Beverley was flown on the night of 23/24 September 1916 by Capt G F Richardson. Twelve Zeppelins set out to attack London and the Midlands. Five of the raiders crossed the Lincolnshire coast between 2200 and 2300 hrs and eventually bombed Nottingham causing few casualties but substantial damage. Capt Richardson took off at 2245 hrs and patrolled from Beverley to south of the Humber, eventually being forced to return by low cloud and fog, thus missing the returning enemy raiders. He landed back at Beverley at 0001 hrs.

July 1916 saw a change in the use of the aerodrome at Beverley. While retaining 'C' Flight of 33 (HD) Squadron, the primary role of the station was turned to training and No 36 Training (ex-Reserve) Squadron was formed. No 33 Squadron moved out in October 1916 to the south of the Humber, to be headquartered at Gainsborough with flights based at Kirton-in-Lindsey, Scampton (Brattlesby) and Elsham. This change to the training role saw a re-equipment in the aeroplane establishment, with Armstrong Whitworth FK 3s, Sopwith 1½ Strutters, Avro 504s, Sopwith Camels and Pups replacing the BE2c and BE12 of the Home Defence units.

In February 1917 after formation at Doncaster, No 82 Squadron was based at Beverley until the end of March. In May of the same year all the Reserve Squadrons were re-designated Training Squadrons, thus Beverley became No 36 TS.

Between January and May 1917 the RFC formed Canadian Training Squadrons in the United Kingdom prior to their location in Canada. As part of this organisation Nos 78, and 79 (Canadian) Training Squadrons were formed at Beverley from elements of No 36 TS. These were followed by Nos 82, 83, 89, and 90, all being based on Beverley for short periods prior to embarkation for Canada where they became the military flying training schools. These units trained on the Curtis JN 4 'Jenny'.

No 60 TS was formed from an element of 36 TS on 7 April 1917 and was transferred to Scampton ten days later. On 1 June 1917 the 8th Wing opened a new Aeroplane Repair Section at Beverley. Another element of No. 36 TS was detached to Thetford from Beverley in August 1917 to form the nucleus of No 80 Squadron. The training role continued until 27 November 1917 when No 36 TS transferred to Montrose to change places with No 80 Squadron, which came to Beverley and re-equipped with Sopwith Camel single-seat fighters in December. In January 1918 the squadron was sent to Boisingham near St Omer in France.

In January 1918 Beverley again was part of the training establishment when No 72 Training Squadron was transferred from Wyton, with Avro 504A/J, SE5 and Sopwith Camel aeroplanes. This unit remained until disbandment in March 1919.

The Quarterly Survey of Royal Air Force Stations, British Isles, dated August 1918, lists Beverley as No 72 Training Squadron Station in the 8th Wing of No. 16 Group N.E. Area with the function of:

(a) A Training Squadron Station (one Squadron), single seat fighter,

(b) A 6th Brigade landing ground, 2nd Class

and showed a total personnel establishment, exclusive of Hostel Staff, of 332, made up as follows:

Officers 18

Officers under Instruction 40

N.C.Os under instruction 20

W.Os and N.C.Os above the rank of Corporal 18

Corporals 14

Rank and File 128

Forewomen 4

Women 68

Women (Household) 22

Twenty five items of transport are listed, including:

Touring Cars 1; Light Tenders 6; Heavy Tenders 6; Motor Cycles and Sidecars 4;

Right: An aerial view looking westwards over Beverley Westwood and the RFC camp.

Trailers 2; one Ambulance and one Motor Roller.

(the general condition of the Westwood even today would make this latter item essential). Twelve SE5s and twelve Avro 504s are listed.

The aerodrome is described as:

> ...having an area of 179 acres, of which 45 acres are occupied by the Station and Racecourse Buildings. The maximum dimensions are 1,150 x 600 yards The height above sea level 100ft. The soil, heavy loam. The surface is bad except for a small area about 500 x 400 yards, rather undulating and slopes towards the north-east. The south-eastern portion of the aerodrome has a very bad surface. The general surroundings are enclosed, with the town to the east. Small fields. Forced landings are difficult.

The Technical buildings on the site were listed as:

> Two Aeroplane Sheds (each 210ft x 65ft)[2] and one Aeroplane Repair Shed (170ft x 100ft).
>
> One Salvage Shed; two MT Sheds; Technical Stores; Oil Store; Petrol Store; Ammunition Store and Night Store.
>
> Workshops: General (130ft x 30ft); Smiths (20ft x 16ft); Gunnery Workshop
>
> Instructional Huts: General Hut; Gunnery Instruction Hut; Photographic Hut.
>
> Offices
>
> Power House; Guard House.
>
> Latrines
>
> Compass Platform and Machine Gun Range

The Regimental buildings comprised:

> Reception Station; Officers Mess; five Officers Quarters; Officers Baths and Latrines; Sergeants Mess; Sergeants Latrines; Regimental Institute; Regimental Store; five Men's Huts; Men's Baths; Men's Latrines and Ablutions. Drying Room and a Coal Yard.

On 1 August 1918 the progress of the works

was:

> Technical Buildings 90%
> Roads 100%
> Lighting- wiring well forward 45%

The estimated date of completion is given as 31 August 1918.

The Survey also reveals some interesting meteorological details of the period. During the winter months October 1917 to March 1918 the following records are given:

> Low clouds 90.5 hours: Rainfall 285 hours: Wind 508 hours: Mist 127.5 hours
>
> Fog 16.5 hours: Possible flying hours 955.5: Total daylight 1,734 hours:
>
> Ratio of possible flying hours to daylight hours 55.10%.

This would not be very different to the local weather at the present day.

With the resumption of horse racing activities in 1922 following the acquisition of land to the north, the old racecourse was changed to its present outline and with the subsequent development of the present day racecourse buildings it is almost impossible to determine what remains of the aerodrome.

[2] The Aeroplane repair Shed listed in the Survey is given the same dimensions as a General Service shed ['Belfast Hangar'] but an aerial photograph dated 7/5/1917 (see page 30) shows that the three sheds were all the same size and each one showed the distinctive pitched roof outliner with two gables at one side. From this evidence it is clear the three sheds were of 1913-pattern Coupled Side Opening Aeroplane Sheds. This conflicts with the Survey. Action Stations No 4 White Rose Base and Balloons to Buccaneers show pictures of an AW FK3 crashed adjacent to the timber door gantry of a 1916 GS Shed, supposedly at Beverley. Recently, however, a pilot's log book has come to light which indicates that the location was in all probability South Carlton, Lincolnshire.

This patch in the grass is the only trace left of one of the aeroplane sheds on Beverley Westwood, now part of the racecourse.

From the study of an aerial photograph dated May 1917 it would appear that the buildings used as the workshop today and the 'Rapid Lad Bar' could be of First World War origin. To the north of the present bungalow dormitory the base outline of one aeroplane shed can be seen in the grass and there is limited visual evidence of another. There is no evidence to be found of the aeroplane repair shed which would have been located in the area of the present parade ring and recently built offices and weighing room. Ground staff at the Race Company tell me that in the area where some of the Regimental site huts were, now the location of the stable buildings, there are many drains that have no function today. There is a gap in the

A Curtiss JN4 'Jenny' used by the Canadian Training Squadrons during their period in the United Kingdom, with RFC and RNAS training units. The machines used in this country were manufactured by the Curtiss Company in Toronto, Canada. Note the vertical camera mounted on wooden rails below the rear cockpit.

This Jonques-built BE2b, 2785, is typical of the primitive early aircraft types used by the RFC. Parked outside a twin Side-Entry shed, the aircraft was in use as a training machine, but where and with which squadron is unknown.

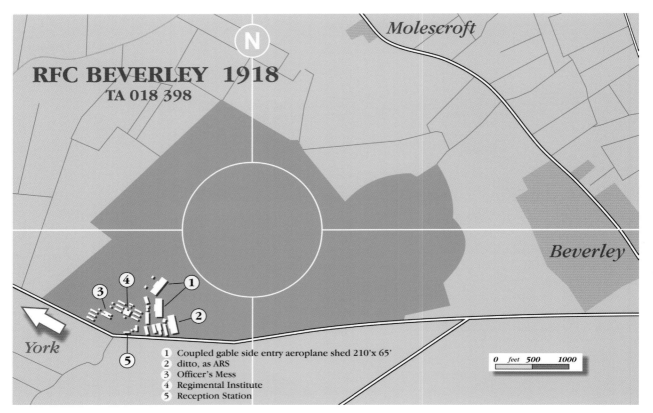

RFC BEVERLEY 1918
TA 018 398

Moleseroft

Beverley

York

0   feet   500   1000

1   Coupled gable side entry aeroplane shed 210'x 65'
2   ditto, as ARS
3   Officer's Mess
4   Regimental Institute
5   Reception Station

roadside hedge with evidence of tarmac about where the entry to the Regimental Site was located. The land used for flight operations would have been in the area to the north of the present racecourse boundary hedge. The only other evidence of the aerodrome today is a brass plaque in the church at Bishop Burton, in whose parish the aerodrome was located, to the memory of the eighteen airmen killed while serving at RAF/RFC Beverley.

The Aerodromes

Eastburn/Driffield

4

As the threat to the British Isles from aerial bombardment was countered by the formation of Home Defence squadrons so the increase in aerial combat over the Western Front gave rise to the need to train novice pilots in the arts of aerial combat. In November 1915 the War Office instructed the Commanding Officer of the Administrative Wing (responsible for training) that as the number of aerial combats were now increasing, the pilots and observers under instruction at home should, as far as possible, be given training in aerial fighting techniques. A suggestion was made that 'trick flying' should be taught. At this time the training of the graduate pilot was in the hands of his experienced squadron peers but as the war progressed training was undertaken at the Home Reserve Squadrons. Training Schools were established to provide specialised training before posting the graduate pilot to an active service unit.

No 1 School of Aerial Fighting was formed at Ayr in September 1917 to specialise in aerial combat tuition for pilots. Similarly, the gunnery training of observers was undertaken at four Schools of Aerial Gunnery that were established between 1916 and 1917. A major contribution to the training of the fighter pilot in the summer of 1916 was the introduction of the Hythe Camera Gun. Made in the form of the Lewis machine gun, film advance was by activation of the cocking handle and the camera shutter was operated by the trigger mechanism. After processing, and if the aim had been fairly accurate, the film showed the image of the target aeroplane overlaid with a graticule. From the known airspeeds it was possible to assess the accuracy of aim and to analyse any errors.

In mid-1916 the Military authorities requisitioned 180 acres from Eastburn Farm and a further 60 from the neighbouring Kelleythorpe Farm to the south-west of Great

In the Aircraft Repair Shed at 21 Training Depot Station, Driffield, this visiting Sopwith 7F1 Snipe (probably E6144) was possibly from Marske or Bircham Newton.

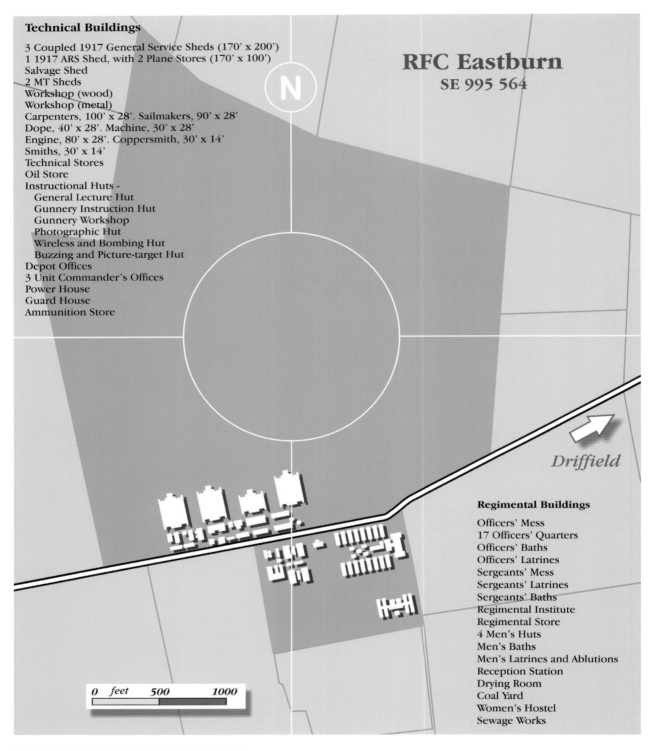

Technical Buildings

3 Coupled 1917 General Service Sheds (170' x 200')
1 1917 ARS Shed, with 2 Plane Stores (170' x 100')
Salvage Shed
2 MT Sheds
Workshop (wood)
Workshop (metal)
Carpenters, 100' x 28'. Sailmakers, 90' x 28'
Dope, 40' x 28'. Machine, 30' x 28'
Engine, 80' x 28'. Coppersmith, 30' x 14'
Smiths, 30' x 14'
Technical Stores
Oil Store
Instructional Huts -
  General Lecture Hut
  Gunnery Instruction Hut
  Gunnery Workshop
  Photographic Hut
  Wireless and Bombing Hut
  Buzzing and Picture-target Hut
Depot Offices
3 Unit Commander's Offices
Power House
Guard House
Ammunition Store

N

RFC Eastburn
SE 995 564

Driffield

Regimental Buildings

Officers' Mess
17 Officers' Quarters
Officers' Baths
Officers' Latrines
Sergeants' Mess
Sergeants' Latrines
Sergeants' Baths
Regimental Institute
Regimental Store
4 Men's Huts
Men's Baths
Men's Latrines and Ablutions
Reception Station
Drying Room
Coal Yard
Women's Hostel
Sewage Works

0   feet   500   1000

Left: A 24-inch gauge Well Tank 0-4-0 locomotive used by the contractors, Matthews & Son, to move building materials to the site from the local railway system. In the background on the compass platform is an Avro 504.

Driffield. Construction work commenced in December 1916 to provide the facilities required for an aerodrome on each side of the Driffield to Market Weighton road. In common with the construction of other aerodromes at this period the building work was carried out by civilian contractors. At Eastburn the work was carried out by H. Matthews & Son Ltd. The raw materials were brought into the area by railway. At the time Driffield was an important railway junction with connections to most of Northern England and two railway lines passed close to the site. Taking advantage of this, the contractors at Eastburn laid down a 24-inch gauge light railway into the Technical Site on which to move the vast quantities of building materials required for the seven aeroplane sheds. This was common practice on aerodromes under construction during this period and from a contemporary photograph a well-tank 0-4-0 steam locomotive, probably manufactured by the Robert Hudson company, was in use. On completion of the work the contractor was required to leave the railway in situ.

This light railway is believed to have been connected to a spur siding on the Driffield to Market Weighton NER line adjacent to Kelleythorpe, where the Driffield Show Ground and the Rugby Club are now. This spur siding is shown on the 1in = one mile Ordnance Survey 'Popular Series' map sheet 28 (with 1924 corrections), but is absent from later editions. This also shows the Technical Site buildings, but not a light railway line.

Previously published books have stated that Eastburn was established as a Home Defence landing ground for 33 Squadron. Recent research shows that Eastburn was not listed in documents held in the Public Record Office as a 33 Squadron landing ground until 1918. It may be assumed that from the dates when the land was requisitioned and construction started, it always was the intention to establish an aerodrome at Eastburn. Another pointer to this view is the fact that the average size of a landing ground in East Yorkshire ranged from twenty eight to eighty acres with an average size of fifty five acres. If it had been intended that Eastburn was to be a landing ground why requisition 240 acres initially and start building the facilities for an aerodrome within six months?

The build-up of the facilities, through into 1917, together with the formation of No 2 School of Aerial Fighting on 11 October 1917, started aviation activity at Eastburn. Under the command of Capt Harold Balfour (later Lord Balfour of Inchrye) the School operated a variety of aircraft: Bristol M1c, Airco DH4, DH9, Avro 504J, Sopwith Dolphin and Camel. Incidentally, it is reported that it was Capt Balfour's daily exercise to fly round the Driffield church tower and see how close he could get to the flag pole without actually touching it... Much later, when a Member of Parliament, it was he who took Maj Draper (the 'Mad Major') to task for flying through Tower Bridge.

The United States of America had entered the conflict in April 1917 but it was nearly a year later that American forces arrived in Europe. An element of this expeditionary force was made up of units of the United States Army Air Service (USAAS). Fifty men of 'D' Detachment, 6th Construction Company, arrived at Eastburn on 12 April 1918. They were joined by men of the 5th Construction Company at about the same time to carry out construction work on the aerodrome. In July fifty

Fifty men from D Detachment of the 13th Squadron of Carpenters were there to carry out carpentry and general building work under the command of Lts Crary and Glaser. These units left Driffield during August 1918. There is no doubt that these units probably give rise to the reports that 'Eastburn was built by the Americans'.

Ground crews from the 25th Aero Squadron USAAS were stationed at Marske for instruction in all aspects of running a unit, while pilots and observers were attached to RAF/RFC operational squadrons on the Western Front. In similar fashion the 263rd Aero Squadron, USAAS, ground staff were stationed with No 21 TDS. Here they were instructed in all aspects of running flying unit. At an inquest in October 1918 two members of the squadron were reported as having tried to rescue the English pilot from a crashed aeroplane. The American unit left Driffield, by train, on 17 November after taking part in the local Armistice celebrations.

On 1 April 1918 the RFC and the RNAS were merged to form the infant Royal Air Force but they continued for many months to operate under their previous management.

Under the new organisation part of No 2 School of Aerial Fighting at Eastburn together with the Marske based No. 4 (Aux) School of Aerial Gunnery were absorbed into No. 2 School of Aerial Fighting and Gunnery at Marske aerodrome, near Redcar. This new school at Marske was then re-designated No 2 Fighting School in May 1918 and trained both pilot and observers in the arts of aerial combat. The remainder of No 2 SoAF, including Capt Balfour, then formed the nucleus of No. 3 School of Aerial Fighting and Gunnery and moved almost immediately in May 1918 from Eastburn to Bircham Newton in Norfolk.

Activity continued at Eastburn and in July 1918 No 21 Training Depot Station (N.E. Area; No. 16 Group, 19th Wing) was formed there by posting in Nos 3 and 27 Training Squadrons from Shoreham and London Colney. The Training Depot Stations were created to economise on both training facilities and land where each TDS specialised in a particular aeroplane type, No 21 TDS was allocated the Royal Aircraft Factory SE5a as its main training machine. Nos 3 and 27 Training Schools were selected to form the new unit as they were already familiar with the type. In July 1919 No 21 TDS was re-designated No 21 Training School.

The aircraft establishment of Eastburn during the period July 1918 through to July 1919 is listed in one reference as Sopwith Pup, SE5a, F2B, DH6, Avro 504J/K, SPAD S7.

In August 1918 the RAF carried out a survey of its assets and these are set out in *The Quarterly Survey of Royal Air Force Stations, British Isles.*

The entry for Eastburn lists the manning establishment, excluding Hostel Staff, as 839, of which the permanent staff comprised 51 officers and 392 NCOs and other ranks. Under instruction were 120 officers and 60 NCOs. One hundred and sixty two women are listed, presumably members of the Women's Royal Air Force, WRAF, as they were known at that time (not to be confused with the later successors to the Second World War WAAF). In addition there were fifty four Household Women.

The unit was provided with one touring car, ten each light and heavy tenders, eight motor cycles and sidecars plus five trailers of undetermined size.

In the Survey the aerodrome is described as having maximum dimensions of 1,200 x 1,050 yards and a height above sea level of 75ft. The soil is loam on gravel and the surface is good and slopes towards the east. The general surroundings are open undulating country with large fields and enclosed country round the town of Driffield begins about one mile to the east.

The Technical site and landing ground occupied some 180 acres on the northern side of the Driffield to Market Weighton Road, the A163 (now the A614), between the Eastburn and Kelleythorpe Farms. The major buildings on the aerodrome were the six General Service

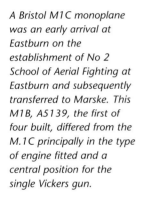

A Bristol M1C monoplane was an early arrival at Eastburn on the establishment of No 2 School of Aerial Fighting at Eastburn and subsequently transferred to Marske. This M1B, A5139, the first of four built, differed from the M.1C principally in the type of engine fitted and a central position for the single Vickers gun.

Sheds coupled into three pairs, a single General Service Shed, listed as the Aircraft Repair Shed. In addition to the Aeroplane Sheds the Technical Site also comprised two MT Sheds; seven Workshops; Technical, Oil and Petrol Stores; Lecture Hut; Gunnery Instruction Hut; Gunnery Workshop; Photographic Hut; Wireless and Bombing Hut; Buzzing and Picture-Target Hut; three Unit Commanders' Offices; Power House; Latrines; Guard House; Compass Platform; Machine-Gun Range; Ammunition Store; Bomb-dropping Tower.

From contemporary photographs the coupled aircraft sheds at Eastburn were of brick construction and similar to sheds constructed at many aerodromes of the period. The coupled 100ft span 'Belfast' trusses, gave

an internal width of 200ft and the assembled length of the sheds was 170ft. The end openings were closed by Esavian Type 120 concertina-folding teak doors that opened onto to L shaped brick end stops and gave an open height of 25ft. From the photographs the internal floors of the sheds were surfaced with concrete or tarmac and the area around the sheds was also surfaced, an original caption to one of the photographs refers to 'the tarmac'.

The Aeroplane Repair Shed was similar in construction but with only one roof truss span, giving an internal width of 100ft, and was the same length as the coupled sheds. Two external annexe Plane Stores, 58ft by 34ft, were built on one side. Unlike the aeroplane sheds the ARS was closed at each end by six

SPAD VII, A9152, and Bessoneaux hangars, probably at London Colney where it is believed that it was on the establishment of No 27 Training School. No 27 and No 3 Training Schools were transferred to Eastburn to form No 21 TDS. Here marked 'T', it appears to have a red and white band on its fuselage.

One of the trio of coupled 100ft span General Service Sheds of post-1918 pattern at Driffield. The sheds were of brick construction with the 'Belfast roof' and Esavian folding doors.

corrugated metal sliding doors. Unfortunately the end supports for the doors are not apparent from contemporary photographs, but it is reasonable to assume that they were built as double-brick arched piers.

An oblique aerial photograph shows that to the east of the aeroplane sheds along the northern road side towards Driffield there were five Bessoneau Hangars. The Eastburn examples appear to have been the 74ft long versions. These are not included in the Survey but are thought to have been erected to provide hangarage during the building construction stage, and afterwards retained on site. Wg Cdr W E Dunn OBE (RAF Rtd), in correspondence dated 1982-1983, recalls that before joining the RAF as a regular in November 1918 he visited the aerodrome at Kelleythorpe on most weekends, where alongside the road to Market Weighton was a line of Bessoneau hangars that were being used to store the salvaged remains of crashed aeroplanes, and where from a friendly sergeant he was able to augment his collection of souvenirs.

The aeroplane establishment listed in the Survey for No 21 TS is given as 36 Royal Aircraft Factory SE5s and 36 Avro 504s (the standard training aeroplane of the period). A collection of contemporary photographs also shows various types of aircraft at Eastburn/Driffield, including SPAD S7, Sopwith Snipe, Airco DH5, Avro 504K. An interior photograph of the Aeroplane Repair Shed shows a considerable number of SE5a machines, stored without the upper and lower outer mainplanes. This album collection reveals that crash landings were not unusual as there are many photographs of SE5as in various unfortunate positions.

The Regimental Site occupied twenty-five acres to the south of the road between the corner where the Four Winds Court Restaurant is now and Eastburn Farm. This comprised : the Mess, seventeen Quarters and Latrines for the Officers; Mess, Latrines and Baths for the Sergeants; four Huts; Baths; Latrines and Ablutions for the Men; the Reception Station; Drying Room; Coal Yard and the Hostel for the women.

These buildings, like the huts on the Technical Site, would have been the standard military sectional wooden huts supported on brick piers. Domestic drainage and sewage was piped to settling tanks to the south-east of the site adjacent to one of the tributaries to the Driffield Trout Stream, a practice that would not be approved of today.

The Survey gives the state of progress on 1 August 1918 as:

> Sheds 65%
>
> Technical Buildings 87%
>
> Regimental Buildings 85%
>
> Women's Accommodation
>
> Roads :
>
> Main roads 70%
>
> Side roads 30%
>
> Water Supply 55%
>
> Lighting 75%

The Survey gives an estimated completion date for the whole station as 1 September 1918.

The civilian contractors held a party for their workers when the work on the site was almost completed. The planned buildings were completed by February 1919, having taken two years construction to complete, but operation of the base had continued during the building, although the projected military personnel numbers were not achieved prior to closure. At this time Eastburn was re-named RAF Driffield to avoid confusion with the RAF aerodrome at Eastbourne in Sussex.

Twenty Reserve (Training) Squadrons had been formed in this country and moved out to Canada during 1917 to form military flying training schools for the infant Royal Canadian Air Force. Nevertheless, training of airmen from the Empire continued at RAF training schools. On 1 March 1919, Lt W.R. Reid, an 18-year old Canadian, took off from Driffield, climbed above the aerodrome and for some reason went into a spin. He then crashed back onto the flying field and was killed. He was given a full military funeral and buried in Driffield Cemetery.

No 202 Squadron, ex-No 2 (Naval) Squadron, having relinquished their Airco DH9 aeroplanes, arrived from Belgium, via Dover, on 27 March 1919 as a cadre. This was a fate that was happening to many squadrons at this period as the RAF, in keeping with the other arms of the Services, was being drastically reduced in size. These squadrons were reduced to cadre status with an official establishment of

Some the SE5as and Avro 504s of No 21 Training Station Depot parked in front of the line of Bessoneaux hangars. The nearest aircraft is a silver-finished Avro 504K. Unfortunately, the serial number is not quite legible.

fifteen: two officers, one senior NCO and twelve other ranks, comprising a mix of various tradesmen. Usually a cadre would have formed the base for a new squadron, but at this time this was the method of running the unit down prior to disbandment. No aircraft were allocated. No 202 stayed until December prior to moving to Spittlegate for disbandment in January 1920. Joining them at Driffield two days later, by the same route from the Continent, the cadre of No 217 Squadron, ex-No 17 (Naval) Squadron, also arrived and stayed until disbandment on 19 October 1919 and subsequent demobilisation.

The first year of peace allowed the home-based units to enter into a more relaxed routine. On 6 June 1919, RAF Driffield held a sports day under the auspices of the Commanding Officer, Maj Murray DSO, DFC. Apart from the usual races, other events were held including 'Tip the Bucket', mop fights, and for the WRAF, an apple race, where they had to run fifty yards, retrieve an apple by mouth from a bucket of water and run back holding the apple in the mouth. An Officers versus Men tug o' war was won by the men. Prizes donated by the Driffield Steam Laundry Company were presented by the CO's wife. During the afternoon the spectators were entertained by the Driffield Town Band.

RAF Driffield/RFC Eastburn aerodrome was not on the list of stations to be retained and

Another visitor to Driffield, this DH5 was possibly from one of the Schools of Aerial Fighting and Gunnery at Marske or Bircham Newton.

Accidents were regular occurrences at the training schools, as with this SE5a, D3433, 'A' at No 21 TDS.

A9152 crashed at Driffield on 11 November 1919 after hitting an adjacent GS Shed roof. This particular aeroplane is reported as having to land at Killingholme with engine trouble on 19 August 1918 while being flown by Lt Coles, RAF, from Driffield. The machine landed at 1030 hrs and left at 1135.

No 21 TS was disbanded in February 1920, when the aerodrome was placed on Care and Maintenance, then being closed down and the buildings finally demolished in 1925. There is no doubt that one of the aeroplane sheds dismantled at the time was re-erected as part of a commercial garage at the junction of Albion Street and Middle Street South in Driffield, and it is assumed that this was the Aeroplane Repair Shed. Unfortunately nothing remains today as it collapsed in the 1940s under the weight of a heavy fall of snow on the roof. Other aeroplane sheds are reported to have been removed from the aerodrome site and re-erected in the district. The author has investigated two sites; one being

Richardson's car showroom in Driffield (now burnt down) and the other an engineering works in Hunmanby, but in both instances examination of photographic evidence and inspection of the sites rule this out.

Nothing can be seen today of the aerodrome Technical Site, as the area occupied by the technical buildings and aeroplane sheds, together with the original landing ground, was incorporated in 1935 into the aerodrome for RAF Driffield. It is still MoD land at the present time, under the control of the Army.

Evidence of the Regimental Site can be found in the field immediately to the west of the Four Winds Court restaurant where there is

The Zeppelin Outrages.

Now that the ban has been removed respecting the publication of news of raids made by Zepps., it may be of interest to recall the fact that Driffield was the first Yorkshire town to have bombs dropped by these murderous machines. The visit was made on the night of Friday, June 4th, 1915, when the machine was seen somewhere in the neighbourhood of the Parish Church about 11 p.m. It was ascertained that it had entered by way of Bridlington, and after reaching Driffield seemed to be in doubt as to its whereabouts. It then cruised round by Langtoft and Slodmere, eventually passing over Driffield on its way home about 1 a.m. on the Saturday morning. Two bombs were dropped, which caused great explosions, startling many of the inhabitants in the town and district from their slumbers. The first bomb was dropped in the garden behind Springfield House, in Eastgate South, doing considerable damage to the root crops and surrounding trees. The houses in the neighbourhood were also much shaken, and some hundreds of squares of glass were broken, while pieces of shrapnel were picked up at great distances from the scene of explosion, and many people received cuts from broken glass. There was only an interval of a few minutes between the explosions, the second bomb falling in a field in Meadow Lane, belonging to Mr. Walmsley, opposite the first gate house, where it made a large cavity, very much resembling a pond, but no other damage was done.

Rumours spread, which were greatly exaggerated, and the town was visited by thousands of people on the Saturday and Sunday, many coming from Hull, who expressed their astonishment at so slight a damage.

Many people had the impression that this visit was one of searching out for a good landing, and this would appear to be correct, for on the following Sunday night another Zeppelin come over Bridlington and Driffield and found its way to Hull, doing a good deal of damage.

This brought the lighting restrictions more strongly into force, and special constables were enrolled to do duty on "Air raid warning" nights, and although we have had many warnings and Zeppelins passing over the town, which caused the inhabitants much worry and anxiety, we have been very fortunate that no further bombs were dropped in Driffield, after seeing what other towns have experienced.

building debris in the ploughsoil zone. An aerial photograph taken in December 1946 shows crop marks and soil stain evidence in the field of several rectilinear buildings and connecting roads. A quantity of broken pottery bearing military crests has been found, probably where there was a rubbish tip. The main entrance to the Regimental Site can be detected where the northern ancient hedge of this field has been replanted. Remains of the sewage works concrete settling tanks, connecting with the domestic quarters, are still visible.

Files and plans relating to the original aerodrome must have been consulted by the Air Ministry in the 1930s under the RAF Expansion Programme as the original flying field and Technical Site formed a major part of the land requisitioned for the new RAF Driffield aerodrome. It is interesting to note that in researching First World War aerodromes, landing grounds and Second World War aerodromes that close co-location of many sites can be found throughout the country.

With press censorship ended after the war, the Driffield Times and General Advertiser was able to publish a report of the bombing of Great Driffield on 4th June 1915.

5 The Aerodromes
Royal Naval Air Station Hornsea Mere

The large size of the Short 184 seaplane is apparent in this photograph of N1274 being manhandled into the Mere from a slipway. Built by Robey & Co, the aircraft was delivered to Killingholme on 1 July 1917, but had been wrecked at Calshot by late September. Despite the rubberised wading suits, the job of the ground crew manoeuvring an aircraft while up to the armpits in cold water cannot have been the most pleasant of tasks.

In July 1914, the RNAS established a naval air station at Killingholme, on the Lincolnshire shore of the Humber estuary, which had facilities for landplanes, but in the main operated seaplanes and flying boats. An Air Acceptance Park was also established on the site. A year later the Admiralty opened a seaplane sub-station under the control of Killingholme to operate from Hornsea Mere. This site, located about half a mile from the coast and separated from it by the town, provided a good seaplane operating area from an enclosed stretch of fresh water, approximately one mile by a half, with water depths varying from about 4½ft to 6ft. The shore based facilities were located on Kirkholme Point, a finger of land at the eastern end of the Mere that allowed launching access into the Mere from its southern shore, and connected directly with the town centre.

Prior to 1917 details of the operations and establishment at the Mere are few as the site operated as a detached unit and personnel and equipment would have been moved in and out of the Hornsea site as required from Killingholme. It is known that Sopwith Schneider, Sopwith Baby and Short 184 seaplanes were based on Killingholme from 1915, so it is reasonable to assume that these types would have made an appearance at Hornsea during 1915 and 1916.

The Sopwith Baby, a single-seat fighting scout seaplane was developed from the Sopwith Schneider, the winner of the Schneider Trophy Race at Monaco in 1914. The Admiralty decided to sub-contract development versions from the Fairey Aviation Co at Hamble and Hayes and George Parnall & Sons at Bristol. These machines were generically known as Hamble Babies and differed from the original mainly in the shape of the fin and rudder. The Blackburn Aeroplane & Motor Company was awarded a contract to modify the original drawings to accept the 130hp Clerget engine, followed by an order for manufacture. Blackburn-built 186 Baby machines, some with 110hp Clerget engines, at their Olympia works in Leeds. The aircraft were delivered by road and rail to the user units until later in the war when No 2 (Northern) Marine Acceptance Depot was established at Brough. At the acceptance depot the machines were assembled, flight tested and then flown to the various service establishments. Many of the Baby seaplanes went to the Air Acceptance Park at Killingholme and then to the user units. The Baby had a wing span of 25ft, a length of 23ft and an all-up weight of 1,715lbs. Fuel capacity gave an endurance of $2^{1}/_{4}$ hours. The maximum speed at low level was 100mph and the time taken to climb to 10,000ft was thirty-five minutes. Two 65lb bombs were carried on anti-submarine patrols over the War Channel off the Yorkshire coast, from Spurn Head to Skinningrove.

By comparison with the Sopwith Baby, the Short 184, a two-seat torpedo, bomber/reconnaissance seaplane, was nearly twice the size. A biplane with a wingspan of

Located on the northern shore of the Point to the rear of the Pavilion structures, the ablutions blocks at RNAS Hornsea Mere have a temporary appearance; not luxurious, but probably a great deal better than on many other stations, and certainly far superior to anything frontline troops in France and Belgium had.

'The Elms' in Chambers Lane in Hornsea served as a billet for officers from RNAS Hornsea Mere in the First World War. The building had changed little in this modern picture.

This is a copy of the 'chart' used by the airmen at Hornsea and the crew members of the airship patrols along the Yorkshire coast. It defines the marked War Channel which was kept clear of mines and patrolled for hostile submarine activity. Each buoy had a particular marker board with an identifying letter. Although the exact meaning remains unknown, in maritime navigation different shaped buoys indicate whether they are to be passed on the port or starboard side. It is assumed that these buoys worked in a similar fashion, thus identifying in bad weather which direction and in which locality an aircraft was travelling. For example, while travelling north the letters on the southernmost buoys spell out SPURN. Going south, buoys spell out FLAMBRO (Flamborough).

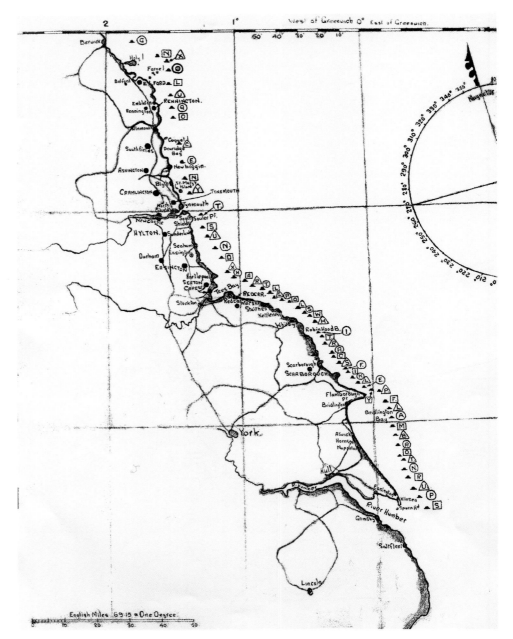

63ft 6ins and length of 40ft 7ins and an empty weight of 3,703lbs, the Short 184 was produced with a variety of engines ranging from the 225hp Sunbeam Mohawk to the 260hp Sunbeam Maori. The weapon load was one 14in torpedo or up to 520lb of bombs carried externally.

Two FBA Type B flying boats were operating from the Mere in 1917. Designed and built by Franco-British Aviation at Argenteuil, the FBA Type B was a single-seat biplane flying boat powered by one 100hp Gnome Monosoupape driving a pusher propeller. Thirteen FBA Type Bs were delivered by rail from Paris to Killingholme during May 1917, and three were allocated to the Seaplane School. Flt Sub-Lt G F Hyams, after his initial training, was sent to the Seaplane School at Killingholme for a 'boat' course and flew the FBA flying boats. He was posted to the War Flight at Hornsea, where his initial flights from the Mere were in FBA 9616, the aircraft that he had brought from Killingholme. Another FBA Type B, 9617, was also at Hornsea by the end of 1917.

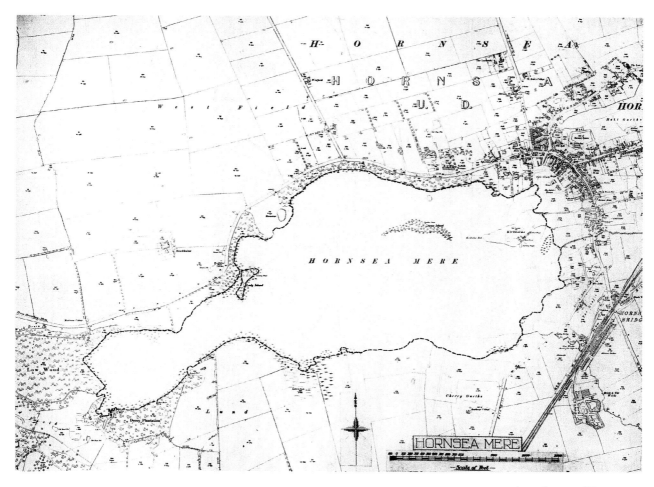

An early map of Hornsea
Mere showing the road to
Kirkholme Point on the east
of the Mere where the RNAS
station was later located.

Two airmen dressed for a
patrol flight walk out to
their machine. The seaplane
to the left is a Short 184
and is believed to be N1647
which crashed at the Mere
on 28 February 1918, killing
the pilot Flt Lt F C Lemon.

Blackburn-built Sopwith
Baby N2089 was delivered
to RNAS Hornsea Mere
during the week ending 23
February 1918. It served
with 453 Flight and 248
Squadron while at Hornsea.
Note the single 65lb bomb
under the fuselage.

This Sopwith Baby resting
on the slipway in front of
the Bessoneau hangars at
Hornsea Mere remains
unidentified. The marking
behind the aluminium
cowling panels may be a
personal emblem (a Scottie
dog?) or may just be
flaking dope.

A head-on view of a
Sunbeam-engined Short
184 on a slipway at
Killingholme.

Blackburn-built Sopwith Baby N1102 was delivered to Felixstowe in May 1917 and flew two anti- Gotha patrols in May and June before being transferred to Hornsea Mere in July. Ten days after arrival at Hornsea it was involved in a mid-air collision with Curtiss H12 'Large America' 8657 and sank after crashing into the sea. The pilot, Flt Sub-Lt FM Bryans, was killed. The H12, built by the Curtiss Co. in Toronto, had been delivered to Felixstowe in mid-December 1916 subsequently making its first flight in March, suffered damage to its lower wings and hull.

Having continued his 'boat' training at Hornsea, Flt Sub-Lt Hyams made his first flight in a Sopwith Baby, N1411, on 1 October 1917. This particular machine had arrived at Hornsea from Killingholme on 23 September 1917 and crashed on 29 October, becoming a total loss. The pilot is not listed. Gordon Hyams was flying Hamble Baby N1467 on 1 November when the engine failed, resulting in a landing on the sea three miles to the north-east of Bridlington. Hyams was unhurt and the Baby was recovered under tow to Bridlington. Eventually the machine was shipped out to the Greek Government in September 1918.

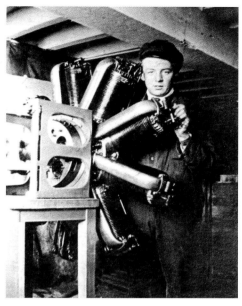

An RNAS mechanic at work on a Clerget 9B 130hp or 9Z 110hp nine-cylinder rotary engine, both types of which were used in the Sopwith Baby.

On 8 November 1917, during offensive operations from Hornsea Mere, Flt Sub-Lt H C Lemon in Fairey Hamble Baby N1469 dropped two 65lb bombs on a U-boat that was 41/2 miles east of Scarborough.

A Short 184, N1647, piloted by Flt Lt F C Lemon had engine failure just after take-off on

A close view of the crew of an unidentified Short 184 armed with 100lb bombs. The aircraft appears to be a completely standard model, but seems to have a fuselage roundel which has acquired an additional white spot in the red centre disc.

A Sopwith Baby armed with a 65lb bomb taxies to a slipway at Hornsea. In the background can be seen the gasworks and the chimney of the brickworks, later the Pottery and now the site of Hornsea Freeport.

Seen on beaching gear outside one of the Bessoneau hangars at Hornsea, this Blackburn-built (at Leeds) Sopwith Baby, N1413, was delivered to Killingholme in July 1917 and detached to Hornsea by October. The large serial numbers on the fuselage side are typical of the machines from Killingholme at this period. On 9 October N1413, while being flown by Flt Sub-Lt Hyams, overturned on the Mere while landing after a gust of wind caused a float to dig in.

A later photograph of N1413 on the slipway at Hornsea, presumably after repairs and repaint. Although not decipherable on the original print the small letters might spell out 'The Jabberwock'.

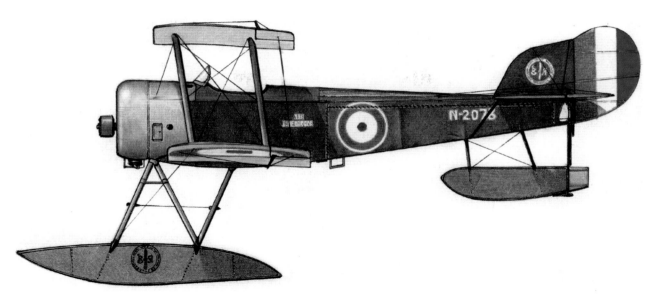

patrol from the Mere on 28 February 1918 and crashed on the south side of the Mere. The observer, Flt Cdr P D Robertson, managed to jump clear just before the machine landed in the marshy ground and caught fire. Robertson, who was miraculously uninjured, went to try to rescue the pilot and was severely burned in the attempt. The pilot was killed and although suffering very severe burn injuries, Robertson survived and was awarded the Albert Medal.

Operating maritime patrols was hazardous in that engine failures were common, often resulting in forced landings on a rough sea, frequently culminating in the loss of crew and aircraft. Several incidents of Hornsea-based aircraft making forced landing following engine failure are recorded. In many cases the pilot was rescued by trawlers in the vicinity. Sometimes the seaplane was taken under tow to the nearest harbour. A common failure incurred during a forced landing by the Sopwith Baby on a rough sea was damage to the plywood floats, which often resulted in the machine overturning and becoming a total loss. In March 1918 two Sopwith Babies made forced landings on the sea following engine failure. N2088 on the 20th, five miles east of Hornsea, was picked up by the steamer *Hans Just* (CT9). The other, N2079, overturned on the 26th following a landing one mile east of Hornsea; the pilot was unhurt and the machine was salved.

Flt Sub-Lt Gordon Hyams christened one of the machines he flew (N2078) *The Jabberwock*. On 26 March 1918, while on patrol over the War Channel, he spotted a U-Boat running on the

surface about ten miles to the north-east of Scarborough. He decided to attack at high speed and low level but was seen by the look-outs of the U-Boat, which then crash-dived. He bombed the patch of foam, but without positive result. Sopwith Baby N2078 had been built by the Blackburn Aeroplane & Motor Co. at Leeds and delivered to Hornsea from Brough on 25 January 1918. There is a replica of *The Jabberwock* in the Fleet Air Arm Museum at Yeovilton[3].

The Royal Air Force was formed on 1 April 1918 by merging the Military and Naval Wings of the Royal Flying Corps. Under the new command structure the 400 series of Seaplane Flights were established. No 404 (Seaplane) Flight was formed at Killingholme in May 1918, equipped with the Short 184 Type Seaplane. No 453 (Baby Seaplane) Flight absorbed the Sopwith Babies of the War Flight at Hornsea on 30 May 1918, and No 405 (Seaplane) Flight was formed at Hornsea on 15 June 1918, equipped with the Short 184. The three flights were under the control of No 18 Group which had been formed in April 1918.

American troops had started to be stationed in the United Kingdom in the early months of 1918 and in common with aircrew members of the USAAS who were posted to operational squadrons of the RFC/RAF, their naval equivalents were also posted to operational units of the RNAS. Lt. DCS Bland USNFC had to make a forced landing on 22 April 1918 in fog, one mile to the north-west of the Mere while flying N2078, *The Jabberwock*. The machine was

Sopwith Baby N2078, named The Jabberwock is finished in the standard clear dope undersurfaces, probably also with the reddish-brown PC12 uppersurfaces typical of many Sopwith marine aircraft. N2078 had an interesting, if brief, career with the RNAS. Delivered to Hornsea on 25 January 1918, it bombed a U-boat 10 miles NE of Scarborough on 26 March while being flown by Flt Sub-Lt G F Hyams. On 23 April Lt D C S Bland (USN) was obliged to force land in fog. Returned to base the following day, the aircraft then formed part of the establishment of No. 453 Flight on 25 May, but was written off on 25 July. The preserved Baby in the Fleet Air Arm Museum is finished in these markings.

[3] Flt Sub-Lt Hyams was one of the earliest recipients of the newly-instituted DFC (Distinguished Flying Cross).

written off, but the pilot was only slightly injured. Ensign Burtchart, another American navy pilot operating from the Mere and flying Baby N1448 on 30 June, crashed on take-off and was injured. The Baby was written off.

The increasing dependency of the United Kingdom on imports of food and materials through 1917, and the threat of unrestricted submarine warfare to coastal shipping, forced the Admiralty into extending air coverage of the coastal shipping lanes with airships (and some landplanes) to augment the seaplane operations. With the formation of the RAF in April 1918, the RNAS training school at Redcar was closed and it was decided to assist the under- resourced RNAS by using the DH6 machines of the training school to carry out trial patrols of the War Channel off the Tyne estuary. Following these trials it was decided to extend the Marine Operations using the DH6.

Nos 250, 251, and 252 (Special Duty) Squadrons were established on 1 May. Each squadron comprised several flights, which were in many cases based on No 6 Group Home Defence landing grounds to extend the patrol area capability. The facilities on these sites were primitive; Bessoneau hangars were provided, the officers billeted locally and the men housed in tents.

No 251 Squadron RAF was formed at Hornsea on 1 May under the command of Maj J D Maude. The Squadron had its headquarters at Hornsea and the Special Duty Flights under its command were based at Atwick (504), Greenland Top (505) in Lincolnshire, and Owthorne (506). These Special Duties (SD) Flights were all formed on

30 June and equipped with the Airco DH6. They were joined in No 251 Squadron by No 510 (SD) Flight from Redcar (ex- No 252 Squadron) in November and now based on West Ayton, near Scarborough.

In July 1918 the base at Killingholme was transferred to the United States Naval Air Service for flying boat operations and all British units were transferred to other bases. No 404(Seaplane) Flight moved from Killingholme to Hornsea. All the three seaplane flights came under the operational control of No 18 Group. Although now part of the RAF these flights still operated as RNAS units with Capt H C Mallet RN in command.

Further reorganisation of the new Service saw the establishment of 79 (Operations) Wing in August with its headquarters at Hornsea and commanded by Lt. Col. F.K. McLean. The RNAS Station on Kirkholme Point was now titled Marine Operations (Seaplane) Station. The new wing controlled No 251 Squadron and the newly formed No 248 Squadron, which comprised Nos 404, 405 and 453 Flights. The Station also came under control of the new Wing.

Flt Sub-Lt Hyams, when returning from patrol on 19 July, spotted the crew of the USNFC Curtiss H12 flying boat, N4336, wrecked on the surface some twelve miles east of Hornsea after a forced landing due to petrol failure. Hyams inflated his lifebelt and managed to drop it in the midst of the crew clinging to the wreckage. He returned to Hornsea, reported the sighting and returned to the site of the crash to lead a Short flying boat to the crash but was unable to communicate with it. He did,

N2113 was another Blackburn-built Baby. It too served with 453 Flight/248 Squadron at Hornsea Mere, which is possibly the location of this picture.

Rigid Airship 25r over Horn-sea Mere while on bombing trials during 1917 to 1918. 25r was based at Howden during the trials.

however, manage to lead two trawlers to the wreckage and the four-man crew of the H12 were rescued. Ten days earlier the same Curtiss H12 had participated in a successful attack on a U-Boat. Hyams was mentioned in despatches for his part in the rescue.

Lt F C Sherwood RN in Sopwith Baby N2095 was successful on 9 August when he sighted and bombed a submarine five miles north-east of Scarborough. Slight wreckage was seen on the surface.

The facilities on Kirkholme Point prior to 1918 are not defined but it can be assumed that they were the same as those existing and listed in the 1918 *Quarterly Survey of Royal Air Force Stations, British Isles* which shows that the Technical Buildings comprised:

Two Bessoneau Hangars

Two Slipways

Workshops (in existing Pavilion)

M.T. Shed

Technical Store

Petrol and Oil Store

Boat House

Power House

Wireless Telegraphy Hut

Guard House

Magazine

Detonator Store

First Aid Hut

Compass Platform

The Regimental Buildings consisted of one Men's Hut as the majority of the personnel were billeted in the town.

On 26 October 1918 the progress of work on the site was:

Sheds	100%
Technical Buildings	90%
Regimental Buildings	100%
Roads, Water Supply	100%
Lighting	85%

An estimated date of completion for the whole station was given as 30 November 1918, but it is understood that the Power House never had the generators installed. The establishment of Hornsea Mere in 1918 comprised:

Personnel	*Transport*
Officers 28	*Light Tenders 1*
WOs and NCOs above	*Heavy Tenders 1*
the rank of Corporal 9	*Motor Cycles 1*
Corporals 3	*Sidecars 1*
Rank and File 80	*Workshop Trailer 1*
Women 21	
Total *141*	**Total** *5*

(exclusive of Hostel Staff)

Machines *Float Seaplanes 12*

From photographs of the period it is possible to determine the location of many of the buildings not shown on the site plan published with the Survey. Entry to the base was by an unadopted road from Queen's Gardens; the

A sailor photographed standing in the pigeon loft doorway dressed in naval 'fore and aft rig'. By repute he was the only serviceman on the station to dress in this fashion.

Guard House was located to the left of the gateway to the site. On the other side of the entrance there were several buildings, presumably where the concrete bases remain. These are thought to have been the Men's Hut and the First Aid Hut. The Power House still stands as the large brick building near the café. The café was listed in the Survey as the existing Pavilion and described as the workshops. Two Bessoneau Hangars stood on the area that is now the Putting Green with two slipways to the Mere. The Pigeon Loft was a wooden hut on the Mere edge beyond the Putting Green. Further to the west along the Point was the circular Compass Platform and further west almost at the end of the Point was a small brick building, possibly the Detonator Store or Magazine. Several boathouses are shown on the site plan along the southern shore between the permanent buildings and the entrance. A boathouse exists between the café and the Mere edge that may be of the period, certainly one is shown on the Survey site plan in that location.

After the Armistice the armed forces started to run down and as a result No 453 (Baby Seaplane) Flight was disbanded at Hornsea on 30 November 1918. No 404 (Seaplane) Flight and No 405 (Seaplane) Flight were transferred to North Coates Fitties, but this part of the Lincolnshire coast was unsuitable for seaplane operations and the two flights were re-equipped with DH6 aircraft until disbandment on 6 March 1919.

In November 1918 No 251 (SD) Squadron was re-equipped with Airco DH9 aeroplanes and continued in service to January 1919 when it was transferred to Killingholme as a cadre and disbanded in June that year.

With the transfer of the operational units Hornsea was virtually closed, but the headquarters of 79 (Operations) Wing continued to 1 August 1919 when military activities ceased on Kirkholme Point.

Eighty years on there is little remaining on Kirkholme Point associated with the RNAS/RAF activities during the First World War. The Café (Pavilion/Workshops), the Power House and a Boat House exist and some concrete base remnants on the Point can be found, some of which can be linked to buildings shown on the 1918 site plan. A bungalow at the corner of Queen's Gardens has been identified by The Fortress Study Group as the Guardhouse, but a photograph dating from the First World War period clearly shows the Guardhouse to be at the gateway to Kirkholme Point in the position recently occupied by The Bungalow/RSPB Reserve Information Hut. Comparison of this earlier photograph with a recent one of the Bungalow shows the layout of the windows and door on the north side to be the same and, from the author's knowledge, the windows in the west elevation match those of the Guardhouse. The Bungalow also had a small kitchen and toilet annexe on the south side and a similar structure can be seen in the 1918 photograph.

This aerial photo dating from the 1920s shows the locations of the main buildings of RNAS/RAF Hornsea Mere at Kirkholme Point:

1 Guardhouse
2 Bases of First Aid hut and Men's hut(?)
3 Powerhouse
4 Workshops/Pavilion
5 Two Bessoneau hangars
6 Pigeon loft
7 Compass platform
8 Detonator store or Magazine.

The approach to the seaplane station on Kirkholme Point, Hornsea from Southgate. The Guard House is on the left and to the right are the Men's Hut and First Aid Hut.

The Guard House with one of the gate guards and guard dog.

The Guard House survived for many years after the Second World War. Towards the end of its life, seen here, and by then known as 'the Bungalow', it served as a shop for the Royal Society for the Protection of Birds. It was demolished in 2000.

To the west of the putting green, if the weeds permit, the footprint of the compass platform for RNAS Hornsea Mere can be seen.

The Bungalow was demolished in 1999. Evidence of the concrete Compass Platform can be found, dependent on the growth of the herbage and a concrete base corresponding to the location of the magazine or detonator store is partially exposed further on at the western end of the point on its southern bank.

Originally intended to be the Generator House and completed towards the end of 1918, the generator was never installed.

6 The Landing Grounds

Places of the night

On the strength of No 504 (SD) Flight stationed at Atwick from the end of July 1918 to November 1918, D.H.6 B3061 was photographed at Killingholme Shore Station. After the war it was sold into civil use and became G-EARJ.

The activities of the enemy intruders that led to the establishment of the Home Defence Squadrons took place during the hours of darkness and thus anti-Zeppelin patrols had to be flown at night with the ever-present risk of engine failure leading to a forced landing. Additionally, adverse weather could lead to an emergency night landing away from the squadron base. Land was requisitioned in the general operating area of each HD squadron to provide an emergency landing ground facilities. Farmland was requisitioned which was to be cleared of livestock or other obstructions when flying was notified and each squadron was responsible for the landing grounds allocated to it.

There were three Classes of landing grounds:

1st Class could have flares set out in any direction, had a good surface and no flight path obstructions.

2nd Class had surface irregularities or obstructions which hampered approaches from certain directions.

3rd Class usually allowed approaches along a single axis and were only taken up when a better local alternative was unavailable.

Some of the landing grounds were Day only but the majority were primarily for Night use, where the Class was identified by the number of flares laid out.

The landing grounds in the East Riding of Yorkshire were initially the responsibility of No 33 (HD) Squadron although latterly the responsibility was also shared with No 76 (HD) Squadron.

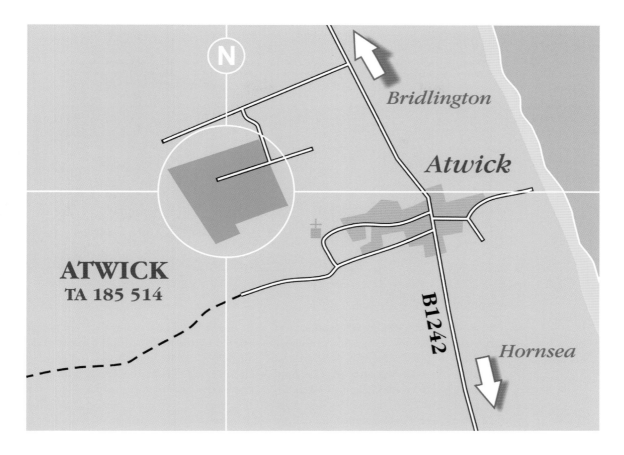

Atwick

The Naval Wing of the Royal Flying Corps opened the facility at Atwick as an outstation for Scarborough/Redcar in July 1915 to support their home defence responsibilities and used the site from August of that year[4].

Very soon after arrival at Atwick the RNAS were called to action on the evening of 9 August when Navy Zeppelin L 9 (*Kptlt* Odo Loewe) appeared off Flamborough Head at 2015 hrs and nosed over the coast twice. The RNAS had already had warning of the intruder and had flown several patrols from Redcar and Scarborough. On the recently opened landing ground at Atwick the pilots were awaiting news of the intruder when L 9 was seen looming through the evening twilight. Flt Cdr C Draper, the CO, and Flt Sub-Lt A S Goodwin took off in a Bristol TB8, 1217, at 2020 hrs and after climbing slowly to 3,000ft found that L 9 had turned about and was now lost to sight in the mist. According to one reference, the Bristol TB8 was 'smashed on take-off', but this cannot have been too serious as the machine was

airborne again later that night. A Blériot XI-2, 3228, piloted by Flt Sub-Lt R G Mack also took off at 2020 hrs but had the same problem locating the raider in the gloom. On return to the Atwick area night had fallen, the fog thickened and Mack crashed trying to land. The aeroplane was a write-off but the pilot was unhurt. On L 9's second intrusion Draper took off at 2110 hrs in thickening mist and climbed slowly to 4,000ft to chase L 9 for thirty-five minutes before losing sight of the Zeppelin. L 9 finally crossed the coast some six miles south of Hornsea at around midnight and was heard at Atwick but by then visibility was too bad to fly a patrol. L 9 flew on across the East Riding and bombed Goole, which Loewe thought was Hull.

The Bristol TB8 was originally designed and developed in 1913 as a two-seat biplane bomber, the first to be specifically designed for that purpose. Powered by a 80hp Gnome rotary engine it had a maximum speed of 65mph, a wing span of 72ft and a length of 46ft. The TB8 had an unusual four wheel main undercarriage. Machine No 1217 was one of a batch of twelve originally ordered by the

[4] One book (The Air Defence of Great Britain 1914-1918) makes reference to pilots at the newly opened Atwick aerodrome on the racecourse north of Hornsea. Searches for this racecourse proved fruitless. Some local knowledge said that there was a 'racecourse field' to the south of the village and to the west of the B 1242 road almost opposite Eastfield Farm. The location given in Royal Navy Aircraft Serials and Units 1911-1919 and other references place the site to the north-west of the village and that is the location shown in the accompanying site map.

Bristol TB8 1217, detached to the RNAS unit at Atwick flew on an AZP on 9 August 1915. The aeroplane is unusual in that the main undercarriage is four wheeled. It also appears to wear the mottled camouflage applied to very early RNAS aircraft. 1217 was struck-off charge at the end of November 1918.

Military Wing of the RFC but the contract was transferred to the Admiralty prior to delivery to the aerodrome at Gosforth, Newcastle in November 1914. On the evening of 14 April while detached to Whitley Bay, 1217 was flown by Flt Sub-Lt P Legh, making his first night flight, with L M B Hinkler in the front cockpit who was armed with a carbine and incendiary bullets. They chased Zeppelin L 9 (*Kptlt* H. Mathy) for one hour and twenty-five minutes without success. Legh had only passed out of the RNAS flying school on 10 March.

The Blériot XI-2 was also a pre-war design supplied by the French manufacturers to an Admiralty Contract and delivered to Redcar in July 1915 and detached to Atwick a few days later. Very similar to the monoplane flown by Louis Blériot across the Channel in 1909, the XI-2 was a larger two-seat reconnaissance monoplane powered by an 80hp Gnome rotary engine giving a maximum airspeed of 75mph. No armament was fitted, the crew being reliant on personal weapons.

The two-seat reconnaissance monoplane Bleriot X1-2, 3228, of 'D' Flight, Hornsea, also flew in the AZP on 9 August from Atwick. The machine was written off after crashing in fog while trying to land at Atwick after a fruitless search. The pilot was unhurt. This picture shows another aircraft of 'D' Flight, 3232, which saw service at Hornsea between 16 July 1915 and December that year. It was eventually scrapped on 15 August 1916 when at Scarborough.

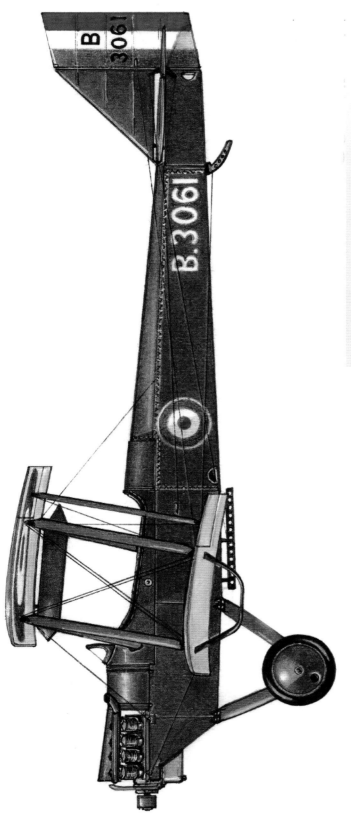

On the strength of No 504 (SD) Flight stationed at Atwick from the end of July 1918 to November 1918, this is Airco DH6, B3061. After the war it was sold into civil use and became G-EARJ, and is seen so marked in the photo on the right. One of the features of the DH6 was that the upper and lower wings were interchangeable, consequently the aircraft tended to carry roundels on the underside of all four wings. On B3061 those underneath the lower wing were very faint. It is possible that an attempt had been made to remove them.

Incident

Barmby Moor was bombed, more or less accidentally, on 27 November 1916 by the two Zeppelins, L 13 and L 22. That same evening L 21 made landfall over Atwick, but was driven out to sea again by guns based at Barmston. The unlucky airship was, however, shot down in flames over the North Sea only a few hours later by the combined efforts of three Norfolk-based naval pilots. There were no survivors.

An Admiralty document dated 1 October 1915 listing the Disposition of Aircraft for the next day on the shore stations in North-Eastern Air Defence shows that:

Redcar had ten of which six were ready

Whitley Bay four, two ready

Scarborough five, three ready

Hornsea (Atwick) four, three ready

Those aircraft based at Atwick are listed as:

BE2c 1117

Blériot XI 3233

Bristol TB 8 1217

Bristol Scout C

On five occasions between September 1915 and February 1916, the BE2c was detached from Atwick to Scarborough, until it was completely wrecked, together with the Bristol Scout, when the Bessoneau hangar blew away in a gale. The Blériot was listed as not ready on 2 October 1915 and was struck off charge on the 2nd.

Under the RFC (HD) organisation Atwick was listed as a 1st/2nd Class NLG for 33 (HD) and 76 (HD) Squadrons. In May 1918 No 251 Squadron RAF was formed and headquartered at Hornsea. Under its control No 504 (SD) Flight was stationed at Atwick to operate DH6 aeroplanes on Marine Operations. These were anti submarine patrols of the War Channel off the Yorkshire coast from the Humber northwards. During this detachment Atwick was listed as an aerodrome. Bessoneau hangars were erected, but only tents were available for the men and the officers were billeted locally.

Atwick had the dubious honour to be mentioned in the account of the last Zeppelin raid of the war on the 5/6 August 1918. 'A' Flight of No 33 (HD) Squadron at Scampton despatched two aeroplanes in response to a spurious report of a Zeppelin six miles off Spurn Head. A Bristol F2B Fighter, C4698, flown by Lt F A Benitz and Lt H Lloyd-Williams took off at 2237 hrs and returned with petrol pressure problems. Benitz took off again 20 minutes later and after a patrol of 105 minutes was attempting to make an emergency landing at Atwick when he crashed on the beach at 0055 hrs. Lt Benitz was killed and his gunner was badly injured. The records contain no reason for the diversion to Atwick.

The DH6 aeroplanes were replaced by D.H.9s in November 1918 and the squadron was transferred to Killingholme the following January. Atwick closed in March 1919.

Barmby Moor

A 2nd Class Night Landing Ground for the Home Defence squadrons operating in the eastern area of Yorkshire. The facility was originally under the control of No. 33 (HD) Sqn and latterly No. 76 (HD) Squadron based in the North Yorkshire area. The landing area comprised 56 acres, giving an operating area of 580 x 430 yards. Located about a half-mile to the north of the A1079 York to Market Weighton road between Wilberfoss and Barmby Moor, the site was opened in April 1916. During the last Zeppelin raid of the war on the night of the 5/6 August 1918, 'C' Flight of No 33 (HD) Sqn, then based at Elsham in Lincolnshire, had flown two sorties against a spurious report of an intruder off Spurn Head. Lt G Cameron and his gunner, Cpl Booth, took off in Bristol F2B C8003 at 2345 hrs and spent most of the next two hours wandering around the sky looking for non-existent Zeppelins. The number of aircraft in the air at the time triggered more alarms and caused more sorties to be airborne. Lt Cameron, while climbing to reach his ceiling of 17,000 ft, reported that he had been fired upon with tracer bullets, probably in the confusion from another Home Defence machine testing its guns. Eventually Lt Cameron landed at Barmby Moor at 0150 hrs. The reason for this diversion to Barmby is not logged, but low cloud ceiling had been reported. There were no hangars or other buildings of note on the site and it was closed to air activity in June 1919 when No 76 (HD) Squadron was disbanded.

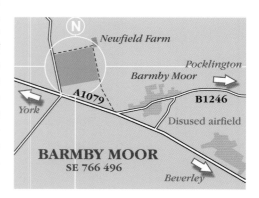

Bellasize

A 1st/2nd Class Night Landing Ground for Nos 33 (HD) and 76 (HD) Squadrons. The site comprised 33 acres, providing a landing area 420 x 380 yards, between Bellasize Grange and the NER railway line from Hull to Goole, south-west of Staddlethorpe junction. References state that the ground was prone to flooding. The landing ground was opened in April of 1916 and finally closed in June 1919. In common with many other sites of this period Bellasize was later requisitioned by the Air Ministry as a relief landing ground, in this instance intended for No. 4 Elementary Flying Training School at Brough, and opened in November 1939. For much of the Second World War, Tiger Moths of No 4 EFTS were a regular sight in the area. The relief landing ground remained open until July 1945.

East Heslerton

No 76 (HD) Sqn opened a 2nd Class Night Landing Ground on the northern edge of the Yorkshire Wolds overlooking the Vale of Pickering. Located to the south of East Heslerton village and about ten miles from the coast at Filey Bay. The precise location of the site is difficult to identify, but is thought to have been on East Heslerton Wold plateau to the western side of the unclassified road opposite East Heslerton Wold Farm. Much of the operating area of the landing ground would have been about 550ft. above sea level. The landing ground comprised 82 acres with operating dimensions of 600 x 600 yards and was opened in 1918. No76 (HD) Squadron. was disbanded in May/June 1919 and the NLG was closed

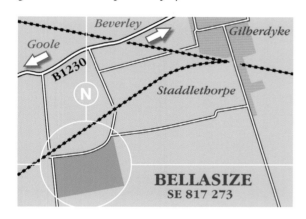

Hedon

Eighty acres was requisitioned in April 1916 on the northern side of the A1033 Hull to Hedon road and to the east of the Preston road junction to provide a 1st/2nd NLG for No 33 (HD) Squadron initially and later No 76 (HD) Squadron. A flying area of 800 x 50 yards was available. Prior to 1914 the site was the Hedon Racecourse. Military use of Hedon finished in June 1919 and Hedon was re-opened as the Hull Municipal Airport in the 1920s. In the 1940s it was the site of an Air Training Corps gliding school prior to its relocation to RAF Leconfield.

Menthorpe Gate

Opened in January 1917 for No33 (HD) Squadron, the 3rd Class Night and 2nd Class Day Landing Ground known as Menthorpe Gate, from the railway station half a mile to the south, was located on the eastern side of the North Duffield to Menthorpe road and just to the north of the NER railway line from Selby to Market Weighton. 67 acres were requisitioned which provided an operating area of 750 x 700 yards. From August 1917 Menthorpe Gate was also used by No 76 (HD) Squadron. The NLG was closed in June 1919. Again the location was used again in the Second World War, but as a decoy site and RAF Breighton was built immediately opposite, east of the river Derwent.

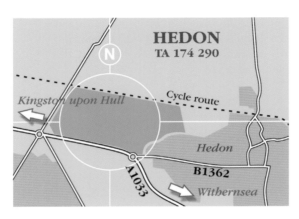

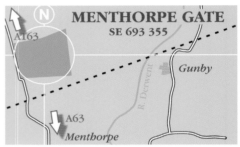

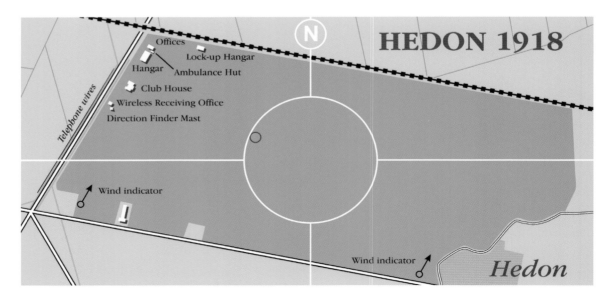

The landing ground at Hedon has changed little from its First World War days. It is shown here with the addition of some small buildings and wireless (radio) equipment dating from the mid-1930s when it became the home of Hull Aero Club and the Hull Municipal Airport.

Owthorne

Another facility for No 33 and then No 76 (HD) squadrons, Owthorne was classed as a 3rd Class Night Landing Ground and may have been initially established by the Admiralty in December 1916. The flying field was to the north side of the B1362 Withernsea to Burstwick road opposite Owthorne Grange and comprised in the first instance 35 acres giving operating lengths of 500 x 250 yards. In June 1918 No 506 (SD) Flight formed under No 251 Squadron to operate from Owthorne with the Airco DH6. To accommodate this increase in activity another 5 acres were requisitioned, increasing the flying area to 500 x 300 yards. Bessoneaux Hangars were erected, tents provided for the other ranks and the officers were billeted locally. Owthorne was then classified as an aerodrome. The DH6s were replaced with Airco DH9s in November 1918. No 506 (SD) Flight left Owthorne in June 1919 for disbandment at Killingholme and Owthorne was closed.

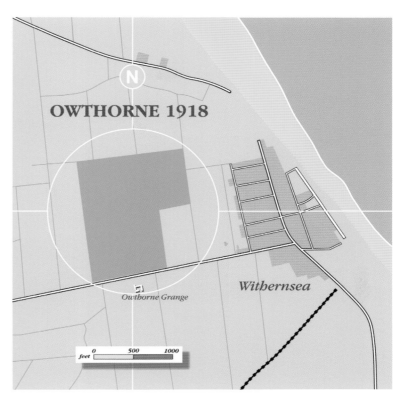

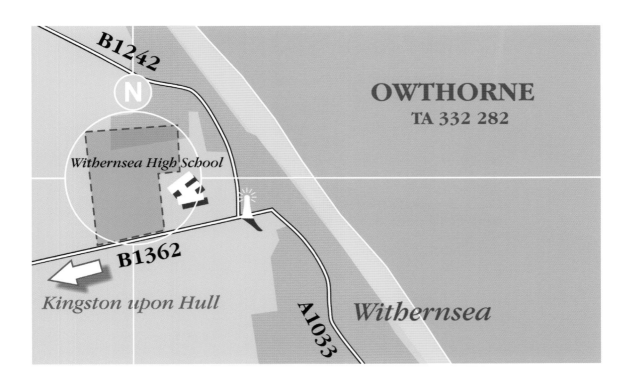

This picture shows a typically anonymous Airco DH6. Unusually it appears to have no rudder stripes, but has roundels on all four wing undersurfaces. Note the massive wooden propeller blades.

South Cave

Taking its name from South Cave railway station, one mile to the south, this 2nd Class Night Landing Ground was located on the western side of the A1034 road from South Cave to Market Weighton and north of the junction of the B1230 to Beverley and the unclassified road to Hotham. The landing ground, totalling sixty-four acres, had an operating area of 480 x 660 yards and was opened in April 1916 for No 33 (HD) Squadron in the first instance and subsequently for No 76 (HD) Squadron. The landing ground remained in use until June 1919. As with other similar landing grounds there is no evidence today from the period.

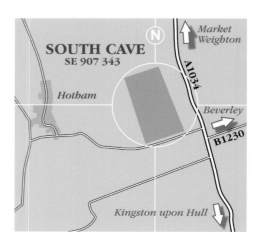

Airship Operations

Royal Naval Air Station Howden;
against the U-boats

7

[5] See chart on page 52

> **Incident**
> *One of the last Zeppelin raids on the East Riding occurred on 12 March 1918 when L 62 (Hptmn Manger) attempted, unsuccessfully, to attack the RNAS airship station at Howden.*

Aerial view of the Station at Howden in August 1918. The road running diagonally from left to right connects with the North Howden to Bubwith road. In the foreground is Coastal Airship Shed No 1, seen looking east. The two large camouflaged tanks are gas holders. Note the windscreen and the supporting framework on the right side of the shed.

Although not a military aerodrome in the same category as those already discussed, Howden cannot be ignored when looking at military aviation activities in the East Riding as, when fully operational by 1918, it was the largest military aviation installation in the area. In fact Howden is considered to have been the most important airship station in the country.

Interest in airships by British military authorities dated back to the early days of the twentieth century. The army's interest was in their capabilities for artillery spotting and battlefield reconnaissance, the navy could see the potential for maritime patrol work. Various early developments of airships were demonstrated to military authorities and some were bought by the army and navy for military development, but neither appeared to have considered the use of the airship as an offensive weapon. In January 1914 the Admiralty took over the responsibility for all military airship activities in the United Kingdom.

Meanwhile, the Germans had realised the potential of offensive operations from the air and their development of the rigid airship (generically known as the Zeppelin) went on apace. When they overran much of Belgium by the end of 1914, bases could be established for the aeroplane and airship, thus reducing the flying distances to this country. Zeppelin attacks against British targets consequently commenced and became a major problem during 1915.

German submarine attacks on allied shipping and in particular against coastal traffic in both the North Sea and English Channel also became a significant irritant. The Admiralty quickly appreciated that a method of defence against the submarine was by armed aeroplanes flying patrols over the coastal War Channels[5]. Ideally the submarine was to be bombed and sunk or at least badly damaged.

The threat of an air attack on a surfaced submarine would, in all probability, cause the crew to crash dive when the attacking machine was sighted and remain submerged for as long as the enemy was considered to be in the vicinity. When submerged the submarine's speed was much reduced, thus allowing surface ships to steam out of range. The airships of the period had relatively low cruising speeds and could spend long periods on patrol. As a result they were considered to be the ideal machine to escort shipping and patrol the shipping lanes. Airships equipped with radio signalling sets enabled naval vessels in the area to be called to the scene when required.

Appreciating a need to establish airship patrol stations throughout Great Britain, in August 1915 the Admiralty despatched to the East Riding two Royal Navy lieutenants, Flower and Burke, to search for a suitable location. By 3 September, the two officers had found that the flat land some five miles north-east of Howden was suitable, in spite of the many drainage waterways. Another factor in favour for the area was the existence of the main line railway facilities, essential for the transport of the building materials and manpower, and later, when operational, the equipment and manpower necessary for military airship activities.

As a result of this survey some 400 acres were proposed for requisitioning, but by 1918 the land under tenure of the airship station had grown to 1,124 acres, stretching from the western outskirts of Spaldington in the east to Brindleys Plantation in the west, with the northern boundary alongside the Wressle to Foggathorpe road and extending south to Brickyard Lane. Following the acquisition of the land by 27 September 1915, construction of the facilities went ahead during the winter of 1915/16.

A single track standard gauge branch line was laid linking the establishment to the adjacent NER main railway line from Hull to Selby at North Howden station. The first airship sheds to be erected were the two designed to accommodate the non-rigid Coastal Class of airships. 'Coastal Shed' 'A' was 323ft by 120ft 5in and a clear height of 80ft. 'Coastal' 'B' had internal dimensions of 320ft by 110ft wide with external annexes along their length. Each shed could hold two Coastal class and one complete SSZ. These sheds were followed by No 1 Rigid Shed, designed and constructed by A Findlay & Co, which had clear internal dimensions of 150ft by 100ft high and 700ft long. The side member 'A' frames provided an internal annexe 35ft wide running the length of the shed. No 1 Rigid Shed was completed in early 1917. In addition to the airship sheds, buildings to accommodate the staff, provide workshop facilities and hydrogen gas making plant (for gas bag inflation) were erected and mains services, water and electricity, were laid in.

The first airship into the new base was Coastal Class C11 which arrived from Kingsnorth on 26 June 1916. C4 also arrived in June by rail for re-assembly at Howden. Both airships made their first operational flights on 3 July. The Coastal Class ships were built at the RNAS Airship Station Kingsnorth near Rochester in Kent. They were non-rigid with an envelope length of 195ft 9in and a diameter of 39ft 6in; the overall height from the base of the

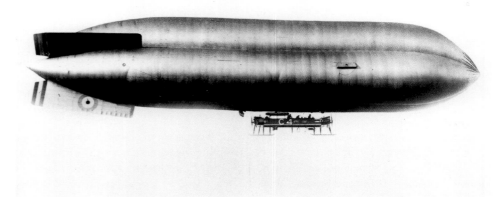

Coastal Class C4 was the first airship into Howden in June 1916. Built at Kingsnorth it was transferred to France in April 1916 and went to the French Air Force. It was then transferred back to Kingsnorth and delivered by rail to Howden. The first operational flight was on 3 July 1916 and C4 completed 1,417 flying hours prior to being taken out of service in January 1919.

control car to the top of the envelope was 52ft. A crew of four were accommodated in an open control car suspended below the envelope. The early version of the control car was made up from the fuselages of two twin-cockpit Avro 510 seaplanes with the tail assemblies removed. The motive source was provided by engines driving tractor and pusher propellers mounted fore and aft on the control car. C11, however, damaged a propeller whilst landing at Howden, thus delaying its first operational flight.

C19 and C21 had arrived by 26 September and were followed by HMA No. 4, originally Parseval PL18, bought in 1912 from the Parseval Airship Co in Germany. Prior to arrival at Howden this airship had been reconditioned at Barrow-in-Furness by the Vickers Co, which had the UK manufacturing rights to the Parseval design. The Parseval machines were the largest non-rigids in Naval service. HMA No 4 had an envelope length of 312ft, a diameter of 51ft and an overall height of 70ft. The power source was two 180hp Maybach engines mounted on each side to the rear of the open control car and driving pusher propellers. HMA No 4 was allocated to a training role at Howden.

By the close of 1916 the complement of Howden was 25 officers and 467 men which included 139 men of the Air Service Construction Corps. In the meantime the airships had completed 521 flying hours in the period from June.

During 1917 the number of airships on site was increased by the arrival of 'Coastals' C4, C10, C11 and also the first 'Rigids', HMA 9r and HMA 25r. The latter machines differed from the other airships on site in that they had a rigid skeletal structure containing the gas bags, the structure being skinned externally. HMA 9r was the first of the large airships into Howden arriving on 4 April. 9r, designed by Vickers' chief designer and his assistant Barnes Wallis (later to achieve fame as the designer of the Wellington bomber and the bouncing bombs used against the German dams) was built at Barrow-in-Furness and was 526ft in length, 53ft diameter and 76ft high. The second rigid, 25r, which arrived on 14 October was slightly larger and had been produced by the Armstrong Whitworth airship works at Barlow near Selby. HMA 25r carried out acceptance trials from Howden and used the Mere at Hornsea for bombing trials. A Vickers-built 'Parseval' ship, HMA 6, delivered for re-assembly at Howden made its trial flight in June and was transferred to the airship station at Cranwell, Lincolnshire, in August. Two more 'Parsevals' were delivered from Vickers to Howden for assembly; HMA 5 and 7 making their first trial flights on 12 November and 22 December. HMA 5 was modified at Howden with the addition of a front gunner's position reached from the gondola by a tubular crawl-way beneath the external envelope. At the end of 1917 the manpower at Howden had reached 40 officers and 612 ratings. A total of 2,086 flying hours had been achieved.

HMA 4 with the original open 'Coastal' control car at Howden after assembly, having been transported there by rail. Originally bought by the Admiralty as PL18 from Parseval in Germany in 1912. HMA 4 was delivered to Howden in December 1916.

HMA 5 was modified at Howden with a nose machine-gunners position known as a 'Howden Pulpit'. It was fitted with a one-off enclosed control car.

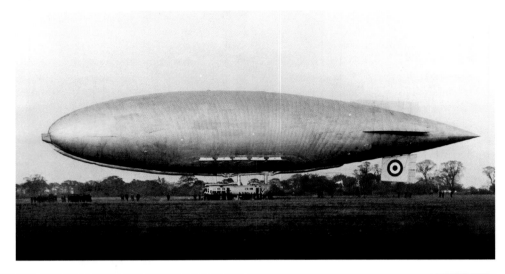

The enclosed control car ('modified Coastal') of the Parseval airship HMA 5 on 12 November 1917. The extensive trunking carried air to the balloonets, while the vertical tube enabled the gunner to reach the 'Howden pulpit'. Note what appears to be at least one 112lb bomb.

A further increase in complement took place in the first months of 1918 when the new non-rigid airships SSZ 32, 38 and 58 arrived and became operational in the March and early April. These were followed by the new Coastal class ships C☆2 and C☆4 replacing some of the old Coastal class ships on site, at the same time SSZ 54 and 55 were flown in. HMA 9r was withdrawn and replaced by a North Sea class non-rigid. At this time the mooring-out sub-station at Lowthorpe was opened to take two of the SSZ ships. A new rigid airship, R27, came to Howden in June, one of the latest '23x' class of rigid airships built by Beardmore at Inchinnan. It was 529ft long by 53ft diameter and 75ft high, but its stay at Howden was cut short on 16 August when a hangar fire destroyed R27, SSZ 38 and SSZ 54. The fire in No1 Rigid Shed was caused when a spark from a W/T set under test set light to petrol fumes in the control car of a rebuilt SSZ. R27 had completed 89 hours flying up to the fire.

HMA 9r at Howden shows the size of the rigids in comparison with the figures on the ground.

Work was started in mid-1918 on the construction of No 2 Twin Rigid Airship Shed. This shed, designed and constructed by Sir William Arrol & Co, was the largest in Britain (and on completion, the largest building in the country) and covered an area of 8.5 acres, including the space required for the doors. Built to house the projected '33' class rigids, the shed provided a clear internal floor space length of 750 ft. Each span had a clear width of 130ft and a clear height of 130ft. The shed had the usual external annexes each side. When completed in 1919 the total weight of the steelwork was 5,208 tons. At the same time

members of the Women's Royal Air Force were posted in to the establishment.

The RNAS was amalgamated into the Royal Air Force in April 1918 and the airship activities became the overall responsibility of the new Service. The personnel became part of the RAF, but the airships and equipment remained on charge to the Royal Navy, a state of affairs that lasted to the closure of Howden in September 1921.

On 6 November 1918 R31 landed at Howden unexpectedly, having left Cardington for its war station at East Fortune, but the wooden structured machine had suffered a

HMA 9r outside No1 Coastal Shed on 5 April 1917, the day after 9r arrived at Howden. Note the large number of men needed to handle the airship.

HMA R26 arrived at Howden in April 1918, direct from her builders, Vickers, at Barrow. The airship was essentially an improved version of 23r. After various trials she escorted the surrendering German submarine fleet to Harwich on 20 November 1918. She was broken up in February 1919 having proved to be probably the first British airship which could be regarded as up to operational requirements.

number of breakages to frames and beams. Remaining at Howden for repairs, R31 was housed in the fire-damaged No 1 Rigid Shed. The roof of this shed leaked following the fire and with the post-Armistice run down R31 deteriorated to an extent that salvageable material was removed and the wooden framework offered for sale in July 1919. The firewood dealer found out too late that the timber had been fireproofed.

Although the First World War ended on 11 November and a general rundown and demobilisation had commenced, Howden continued to be an important unit in the UK airship activities. The last of the Coastal Class, C5 and C9, were withdrawn and replaced by C☆6, ☆7, ☆9, and ☆10 which were on the establishment through to early 1919. SSZs continued to operate from Howden and the mooring-out stations. Three of the North Sea class were known to have been operational at Howden during the year. As Howden had the new Twin Rigid Shed it was considered to be a major unit, along with Pulham and East

Fortune, and escaped much of the post-war rundown. Although the SSZ machines were removed, they were replaced by the 'SS Twins' SST-3, -4, -5, -7, -9, -10, -11, and -12 which were used to assist with the clearance of the extensive North Sea minefields.

By the end of 1919 the airship was considered to be redundant and too expensive for operations and as a result military airship activity suffered drastic cut-backs. Most of the airship fleet was deleted between August and September of that year. On account of its strategic location and the huge Twin Shed, Howden stayed in business, albeit on a much reduced scale.

In a bid to accelerate their rigid airship capability, the Americans decided to purchase the R38 which was being constructed by The Royal Airship Works (the successors to Shorts) at Cardington. R38 was to be re-designated USN ZR2. A naval contingent was sent to Howden for training on rigid airship construction, maintenance and operation and was initially trained on SSE-3, an experimental twin-engined version of the SS Zero class,

The North Sea class of coastal patrol airships entered service in 1917 and were stationed at East Fortune and Longside in Scotland. Many passed through Howden on delivery. The trilobe envelope of this visiting ship is apparent in this photograph taken at Howden.

Developed from the 'Coastal' class of ships the Coastal Star class started to arrive at Howden with C☆1 seen here while on her delivery flight to East Fortune in February 1918. C☆1 was followed by C☆2 in March which remained at Howden until scrapped in 1919.

brought to Howden on 8 March 1920. R32 was also allocated in the same month for rigid airship training. R33 was put into Howden for overhaul in 1920, following which it was permanently homed at Cardington from July 1921. R34 had made the first double crossing of the Atlantic in July 1919 and was permanently assigned to Howden in March 1920, eventually being broken up in early 1921 following damage after a collision with high ground on the North Yorkshire Moors and being moored out at Howden in strong winds. R80 had arrived at Howden in February 1921, but was deflated on arrival as the airship

activities were being run down. The Americans required a metal framed airship for training purposes rather than the wooden R32 and as the metal R34 was no longer available, R80 was reprieved and returned to airworthy condition. Between March and June 1921 at least four training flights totalling over eight hours were made. Following these R80 returned to Pulham making its final flight.

R38 was completed at Cardington and arrived at Howden for further trials on 17 July 1921. On completion it left Howden for Pulham on 23 August with a mixed British and American crew, having been repainted and

SSE-3 being used by an American unit for training at Howden during 1920 while they waited for the ill-fated R38 to be completed.

carrying its American designation ZR2. It was intended that following this fourth test flight R38 would then be prepared for delivery to the United States. Pulham was found to be fogbound on arrival so a return to Howden was made. After cruising off the East Coast overnight R38 was observed over the River Humber, where it broke up into the river at 1737 hrs, just off the Victoria Pier in Hull, with

the loss of forty-four members of the crew, including sixteen Americans. There were five survivors. The loss of the R38 stopped all military airship development in the United Kingdom. Howden closed for military airship operations on 21 September 1921 when R80 departed for Pulham with the Station Commanding Officer on board.

An American unit ground handling SSE-3 and its open car at Howden.

The enormous size and complexity of the Twin Rigid Airship Shed at Howden can be gauged by comparison with the railway trucks just in front of it.

SSZ 63 was delivered to Howden in May 1918 (which was probably when this picture was taken) and was at Lowthorpe later the same month. It made its last flight in June, being later damaged in the fire in No 1 Rigid Shed at Howden on 16 August 1918.

Howden was reopened in 1924 by The Airship Guarantee Co, a subsidiary of Vickers, for the construction of a civil passenger carrying airship. In the 1930s the huge twin shed was dismantled and sold for scrap. The southern part of the original flying area, now a golf course, was used as a practice bombing range during the Second World War.

Lowthorpe

By early in 1918 the Airship Station at Howden was becoming overcrowded with airships so the Admiralty established mooring-out sub-stations for the coastal patrol airships based at Howden at Kirkleatham, near Redcar, and Lowthorpe, some seven miles to the north-east of Eastburn and about the same distance from Bridlington. Lowthorpe should not be confused with the Emergency Landing Ground of the Second World War at Carnaby. The opening of these sub-stations in April and May 1918 not only helped the overcrowding but more importantly reduced the distance from Howden to the patrol areas of the North Sea. Church Wood at Lowthorpe was an ideal location, being only five minutes from the coast at Bridlington Bay by airship. A mooring-out station was usually a clearing in a wood, or in a sheltered location, to accommodate two non-rigid airships of the SS (Submarine Scout) or the SSZ (Submarine Scout Zero) class, which by then were the main machines used to patrol coastal waters. Facilities on the mooring-out stations were primitive; the other ranks were housed in tents and it is likely that officers were billeted locally.

The non-rigid SSZ airships or 'blimps' operated by the Royal Navy were what can best be described as streamlined balloons with cruciform control surfaces, steered from a three-place control car or gondola suspended below the envelope. The crew seated in the control car comprised the pilot, a wireless telegraphist, and an engineer. Mounted at the rear of the control car, the motive power was from a Rolls-Royce Hawk 75hp water cooled engine, specifically designed for airships, driving a pusher propeller.

This airship mooring block removed from Lowthorpe is one of the few relics of the airship era in East Yorkshire to survive. Presently it is in the Yorkshire Air Museum at Elvington.

Cylindrical fuel tanks were attached to the envelope well clear of the gondola. The envelope of 70,000 cu ft contained two hydrogen-filled balloonets of 9,8000 cu ft and the overall shape was maintained by air taken from the propeller sl ipstream by a fixed duct to the rear of the propeller. The overall length of the SSZ ships was 143ft 4in, with an envelope diameter of 39ft 6in. The overall height from the base of the car to the top of the envelope was 47ft. Given these dimensions and the requirement to hold two airships with room to manhandle them to and from the flying field required a clearing of considerable size and at some of the mooring-out stations the airships were moored in the lee of a wood.

The first airships, SSZ 38 and SSZ 32, arrived at Lowthorpe in April 1918. The latter under the command of Capt G F Meager RN, who made his first flight from Lowthorpe on 9 May and after a flight of 9 hours 10 minutes landed in a field covered in buttercups alongside Church Wood. SSZ 38 was damaged on May 10 while being manhandled out of the clearing and was blown into the trees by the wind and deflated.

On 17 May 1918 Meager, who had been recalled from patrol with SSZ 32, decided to pay a visit to the recently established RAF training station at Eastburn, No. 2 School of Aerial Fighting, to take the Commanding

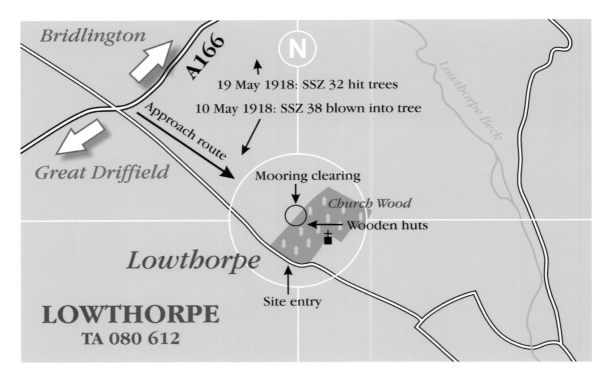

Tented accommodation for the 'other ranks' in the corner of the living field at Lowthorpe.

Officer, Capt Harold Balfour (later Lord Balfour of Inchrye) for a flight. Capt Meager had already met Balfour, who was known to indulge in low level flying, when he had visited Howden with a Sopwith Camel squadron. He indulged his passenger with some low flying 20ft above the roof tops at Driffield and then continuing over the aerodrome where the airship carried away the aerodrome telephone wires in the process! Following this, in the afternoon, two officers from Driffield, who had missed the morning fun, arrived at Lowthorpe by road and requested a flight. Capt Meager obliged and the party was flown back to Driffield at, or below, the height of the telephone wires along the road side. At Driffield the flight continued at low level, narrowly missing the chapel spire by a foot and continued on to the CO's house where it is admitted that they were pretty low as they had to zoom up to miss the house and then to fly through a gap in a hedge. In the course of this more telephone wires were carried away.

On 19 May, after two flights totalling 12 hours 5 minutes, Capt Meager landed back at Lowthorpe on a calm evening at 1940 hrs and decided to give the ground crews flights of ten minutes round the field. After several trips another ship, SSZ 23, was approaching the field and Meager, concentrating on watching it, failed to notice the clump of trees growing on the Fox Hill tumulus, to the north-east of the landing ground. As a result the control car was badly damaged and SSZ 32 had to be deflated, dismantled and returned to Howden by road.

SSZ 32 was replaced with SSZ 63 until 1 June when it was replaced by SSZ 54. On 2 June, while manhandling SSZ 54 out of the clearing, the wind blew it onto the trees and damaged the envelope. This involved dismantling, packing, and road transport to Howden and another Court of Enquiry. Capt Meager's career was clearly not harmed by these mishaps as he was appointed CO of the mooring-out station at Kirkleatham and also to the command of the crew nominated to go to Italy to collect the semi-rigid 'M' type airship that had been acquired by the Admiralty.

Altogether six SSZ class airships were based at Lowthorpe, but there was interchange and visits by other machines from Howden and Kirkleatham.

Nothing remains at Church Wood today except the path through the wood, which was probably there before the airships. Accommodation for the personnel at the site was in bell tents located to the north-east of the wood. The precise location of the clearing for the two airships is open to debate, but it would seem to be sensible for it to have been on the south-west side of the wood to the north of the church. Mr Constable of Ruston Parva, who was born at the New Inn on the A 614, remembers the airships operating from Lowthorpe and some wooden huts in Church Wood. He also saw gas cylinders on a trailer by the roadside. A mooring ring set in a concrete block was removed from Church Wood and is now in the Yorkshire Air Museum at Elvington near York. There are still trees on the Fox Hill tumulus.

A view of the entrance to the mooring-out site in Lowthorpe Woods where the nose of an SSZ ('Zero') Class airship can just be made out. The gap was re-planted with trees in 1920.

In this view looking east towards the church and Lowthorpe Woods, little evidence remains today of Lowthorpe's role in the First World War.

Military Support Facilities

8

No.2 (Northern) Marine Acceptance Depot, Brough

Above: An aerial view of the Blackburn Works at Brough in the early 1920s. To the left are the 'North Sea Sheds'. In the centre is 'A' Shed where the large flying boats were built. On the right and closest to the Humber is the original 1916 shed and slipway. The dates for the large sheds are not known, but they were probably erected as part of No 2 (N) MAD in 1917-1918. Later the site was used as the Experimental Shop, but is now part of a Machine Shop complex. (BAe Systems)

Not part of the Home Defence organisation, the Brough site was established in 1916 by the Blackburn Aeroplane & Motor Company as an assembly and flight test base, initially for seaplanes and flying boats. Robert Blackburn had an interest in seaplanes as well as landplanes, as had many of the other early aviation pioneers. In 1914 the Blackburn Improved Type 1 machine was rebuilt with floats and was then known as the Land Sea Monoplane and operated as a floatplane trainer on Lake Windermere until April 1916. The Blackburn Type 'L', the first biplane to be built by the Company, was entered for The Circuit of Britain seaplane race scheduled for 10 August 1914 but world events meant that the race was cancelled and all the entrants were commandeered by the Admiralty. The Type 'L' was taken to the Blackburn hangar at Scalby Mills, north of Scarborough, and flew several reconnaissance

sorties before being written off in a crash in early 1915. Blackburn continued to design and develop other seaplanes, namely the TB, SP and the GP. Building these machines at the Olympia Works in Leeds required long journeys by road or rail to launch and test. It was decided to find a suitable base from which maritime activities could be undertaken that was relatively near the Leeds factory and a site was found at Brough on the river Humber.

From May 1916 work was concentrated on Admiralty sub-contracts for the manufacture and supply of Sopwith Baby seaplanes. By this

N113 was the first of three Blackburn Blackburd torpedo bombers built in 1918. After torpedo-dropping trials at Brough, it was delivered to Martlesham Heath where it crashed on 2 July 1918.

date the Sopwith factory, with limited capacity, was committed to the first production of Sopwith 1½ Strutters. The first seventy machines were built at Leeds in three batches and delivered by road and rail to RNAS stations for assembly and test. At Brough an assembly shed and slipway were built and completed in time to allow the assembly and testing of the second Blackburn GP seaplane, No 1416. On completion it was delivered to the Experimental Design Flight at Grain, Kent, later in the same year. Manufacture of the Blackburn- built Sopwith Babies continued at Leeds and 115 were delivered to Brough for erection, test and delivery to the user stations.

Early in 1917 the Admiralty took over the site at Brough as an Acceptance Depot. Despite the naval takeover, the site continued to be operated by the Blackburn company with civilian staff. In addition to the original Blackburn shed and slipway, two large sheds, known for many years as North Sea and 'A' Sheds, were erected. A second slipway near the new sheds was built, the date is uncertain. In addition to these sheds a complex of huts was erected on each side of

Skillings Lane to the south of the railway line and the goods sidings (coal yard).

The common practice of the period for the acquisition of Military hardware was by sub-contract. Many manufacturing organisations were engaged to build aeroplanes to main contractor's designs. Phoenix Dynamo Manufacturing Co. of Bradford (later to be part of English Electric), George Robey & Co of Lincoln and The Brush Electrical Engineering Co Ltd. of Loughborough were all sub-contracted to manufacture various designs of seaplane, which were then transported to the various Acceptance Depots by road and rail, assembled, flight tested and delivered to the user stations. In mid-1917 the Phoenix Company was building under contract the Short 184 seaplane and they approached the Admiralty for permission to use the facilities at Brough for final assembly and testing. Between July and October 1917 seven Short 184 were tested by Blackburn test pilots and delivered from Brough.

The Admiralty established No 2 (Northern) Marine Acceptance Depot at Brough in April 1918, with a sub-station at South Shields and a detachment at Dundee. The function of the site

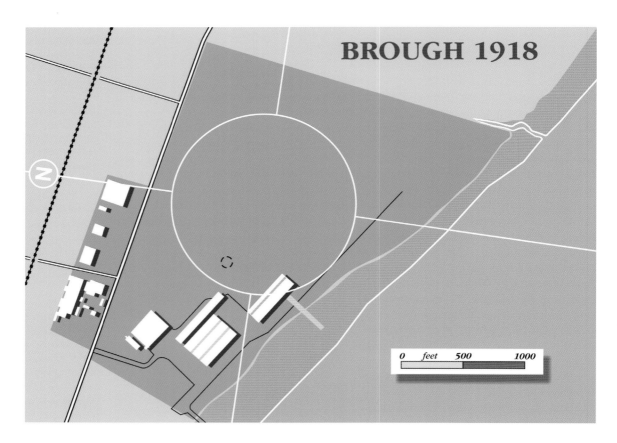

BROUGH 1918

0   feet   500   1000

after the change of name remained the same and was, as far as is known, still civilian manned, although there is evidence in contemporary photographs of naval personnel on site. Seaplanes and flying boats delivered by road and rail from manufacturers were assembled, flight tested, accepted for service use and then delivered to the user establishments. Brough

Felixstowe F 3 N4413 was built in Bradford by Phoenix Dynamo and is seen here on the slipway at Brough in late June 1918. Subsequently it served with 347 Flight and 238, 234 and 235 Squadrons.

Soon after the Blackburn works had been commandeered by the Admiralty, the company was given the task of erecting Phoenix-built Short 184 floatplanes. This is one of them, pictured at Killingholme. It is almost certain that it had earlier passed through Brough and probably also visited Hornsea.

then became the major unit for the acceptance of marine aeroplanes built in the area. Twenty Short 184 machines built in Lincoln by George Robey & Co were delivered through Brough, as were five of the same type built by the Brush Electrical Engineering Co in Loughborough. The Phoenix Dynamo Manufacturing Co had been sub-contracted to build flying boats to a Felixstowe design and a total of thirty-five of these large machines were brought to Brough for assembly and flight testing. After acceptance they were flown to the service units.

The Phoenix Dynamo Manufacturing Co had by mid-1918 established a design capability and had started the development of a flying boat based on the Felixstowe hull design, the type at first designated the P 5, later called the Cork. Two Phoenix Cork P 5 flying boats were assembled and tested at Brough. The first, N86, a Mk I, made its first flight on 4 August 1918 and N87, a Mk II, first flew on 28 March 1919.

While the site was being used as No 2 (Northern) Marine Acceptance Depot the Blackburn Company were using Brough

through 1918 to assemble and test 20 production Blackburn Kangaroos and three Blackburn Blackburd landplanes. After flight test the machines were wheeled over to No 2 MAD for acceptance and delivery.

No 2 (Northern) Acceptance Depot continued in business after the Armistice, although a precise date of its closure is not known, but discussions were held in late 1919 between the Military Authorities and the Beverley Rural District Council to take over the huts for temporary housing. This was stopped when the Blackburn Company indicated a wish to purchase the whole site and this was completed early the following year.

Surrounded by interested workers, this is Felixstowe F 3 N4404, one of 30 built by Phoenix and delivered to 2(N) MAD. This picture shows the flying boat on the slipway at Brough, probably shortly after it was delivered in April 1918. Unfortunately its service career was very brief for it hit a submerged object while taking off on 23 May and was subsequently written off.

Another view of the prototype of the peculiar Blackburn Blackbird showing its complex undercarriage. Note the many fabric-covered struts.

A magnificent picture of Baby N1123 immediately after completion on the slipway at Brough. The quality of the workmanship is apparent in the pristine finish.

1 Appendix One

Units and Representative Aircraft at East Riding Aerodromes

An excellent picture of the instructor (front) and pupil in an Armstrong-Whitworth FK3, 5509, as the ground crew prepare to swing the propeller. It is not known for certain which unit(s) this aircraft served with, but as 5508 is known to have served with No 47 Squadron at Beverley in early 1916, it is believed 5509 also belongs to that unit. It is typical of those used for training in the East Riding.

Beverley

No 47 Squadron, RFC:
> AW FK3: 6226
> BE2c: 2720
> Avro 504A: 7737
> Bristol Scout D: 5570

No 33 (HD) Squadron, RFC, 'C'Flight:
> BE2c: 2661
> BE12: 6661
> Bristol Scout D: 5571
> Avro 504: E3033 (on strength, possibly at Beverley)

No 80 Squadron, RFC:
> Various aircraft

No 78(Canadian) Training (Ex-Reserve) Squadron:
> Curtiss JN4: C122

No 79(Canadian) Training (Ex-Reserve) Squadron:
> Curtiss JN4: C712

No 82(Canadian) Training (Ex-Reserve) Squadron:
> Curtiss JN4

No 83(Canadian) Training (Ex-Reserve) Squadron:
> Curtiss JN4: C476

No 36 Training (Ex-Reserve) Squadron:
> Curtiss JN4: B1942
> BE12a: A4011
> AW FK3: 5553
> BE2c: 2715
> Sopwith 1½ Strutter: A6046
> Sopwith Pup: C288
> Sopwith Camel: B7321
> RE 8: B5029
> Avro 504J: B4204
> Avro 504K: D5295

The office. This is the cockpit of an SE5a, many of which were used for training by East Yorkshire-based units. The spade grip on the control column in the foreground is of interest as it is more typical of those fitted to most RAF fighters up to, and including the Second World War. Apart from the many protruding instruments which offered plenty of scope for damage to the pilot in the event of a crash, the empty box, which was intended to hold a magazine for the over-wing Lewis gun, is worthy of note.

This pristine, but sadly unidentified Wolseley-engined SE5a is typical of many used by the various training squadrons at Beverley and Driffield. Probably taken at Farnborough, the picture gives a very clear view of a compass-swinging platform of the period in original condition. A Side-Entry Shed can be seen in the left background.

No 60 Training (Ex-Reserve) Squadron:
(Formed out of part of No. 36 TS at Beverley for one week)

No 72 Training Squadron:
SE5a: E5389
Sopwith Camel: B9186
Avro 504A: D6272

A Sopwith Baby sheltering in one of the Bessoneau hangars at Hornsea Mere acts as a backdrop for this anonymous RNAS pilot and mechanic. Note the brass sheathing to the propeller blade tips.

Eastburn/Driffield

No 2 School of Aerial Fighting:
AW FK8: B252
DH4: B5224
DH9: C1184
Sopwith Camel: B5582
Avro 504A: B8617
AW FK3: B9594
Sopwith Dolphin: C3854
Bristol M1C: C4995

No 21 Training Depot Station:
SE5a: E5920
SPAD SVII: A9152
D.H.6: A9564
Bristol F2B: C902
Avro 504K: E3658

Hornsea

Pre-April 1918, a sub-station to Killingholme:

War Flight:
Sopwith Baby: N1413
FBA Type B: 9616
Short 184: N1830
Post April-1918:

No 248 Squadron

No 404 (Seaplane) Flight:
Short 184: N2922

No 405 (Seaplane) Flight:
Short 184: N1226

No 453 (Seaplane) Flight:
Sopwith Baby: N2078

No 251 Squadron:
Headquarters staff only

No 79 (Operations) Wing:
Headquarters staff only

Sopwith Baby N2099 was built by Blackburn under contract in late 1917. Originally delivered to Killingholme (which is probably the location of this picture) it later served at Seaton Carew and South Shields before ending its service with 453 Flight/248 Squadron at Hornsea at the end of the war.

Atwick

Classed as an aerodrome post-1918

RNAS (HD) Detached ex-Redcar/Scarborough for AZP:
Bristol TB8: 1217
Blériot XI-2: 3228

No 251 Squadron, RAF

No 504(SD) Flight:
DH6: B3061
DH9

Owthorne

Classed as an aerodrome post-1918

No 251 Squadron, RAF
No 506 (SD) Flight:
DH6: B3096
Sopwith Pup: B2218

Howden

RN Airship Station
Rigid airships: HMA 9r, R38
Coastal Class: C 11, C(2)
Parseval: HMA 4
North Sea Class: NS 1
Sea Scout Zero: SSZ 32
Sea Scout Experimental: SSE 3
Sea Scout Twin: SST 12
USNAS Airship Training Detachment

Lowthorpe

Airship Mooring-out Station for Howden
Sea Scout Zero: SSZ 63

Brough

Blackburn Aeroplane & Motor Company, Assembly and Flight Test facility:
Sopwith Baby: N1123
Blackburn Kangaroo: B9971
Blackburn Blackburd: N113
Phoenix P 5 Cork: N86

No 2 (Northern) Marine Acceptance Depot:
Felixstowe F3: N4413
Short 184: N9140

2 Appendix Two
Known casualties from Zeppelin raids on Hull

These details are extracted from the original police reports and other contemporary documents in certain cases it is unclear whetner victims were killed or only injured. (Reasearch by Barry Ketlty)

6 June 1915 (L 9, *Kptlt* Mathy)
Killed (24)

Name	Age	Location and remarks
William Watson	67	21 Edwin Place, Porter Street
Mrs Watson	?	21 Edwin Place, Porter Street
Mrs Canningham	?	22 Edwin Place, Porter Street
Emma Pickering	68	2 Sarah Ann's Place, Porter Street
Maurice Richardson	11	50 South Parade
Violet Richardson	8	50 South Parade
George (William?) Walker	63	2 St Thomas's Terrace, Campbell Street
Alice Walker	30	2 St Thomas's Terrace, Campbell Street
Millicent Walker	17	2 St Thomas's Terrace, Campbell Street
Mr A. Johnson	?	2 St Thomas's Terrace, Campbell Street

Name	Age	Location and remarks
E Jordan[6]	10	11 East Street, Church Street
Mr Hill	47	12 East Street, Church Street
Mrs Hill	45	12 East Street, Church Street
Florence White	30	3 Walter's Terrace, Waller Street
Isaac White	3	3 Walter's Terrace, Waller Street
Eliza Slade	55	4 Walter's Terrace, Waller Street
One man	(unidentified)	6 Blanket Row
Two boys	(unidentified)	39 Blanket Row
Johanna Harman	67	93 Arundel Street; 'died from shock' 7/6/15
Hannah Mitchell	42	8 The Poplars, Durham Street; 'died from shock' 7/6/15
Elizabeth Foreman	39	37 Walker Street; 'died from shock' 7/6/15
Ellen Temple	50	20 St. James Square; 'died from shock' 8/6/15
Sarah Ann Scott	36	8 The Poplars, Durham Street; 'died from shock' 8/6/15

Injured (27+)

Name	Age	Location and remarks
Arthur Kitchen	49	11 Walker Street
Mrs Needler	?	102 Great Thornton Street
Mrs Walker	?	2 St Thomas's, Terrace, Campbell Street
May Walker	18	2 St Thomas's Terrace, Campbell Street
Mrs Bick	?	St Thomas's Terrace, Campbell Street
One boy (unidentified)	?	39 Blanket Row
Five persons (unidentified)		High Street
'Several' persons (unidentified)		St. Paul's Avenue, Church Street
Six (unidentified)		Edwin Place, Porter Street
Mr Jordan	35	11 East Street, Church Street
Mrs Jordan	32	11 East Street, Church Street
Four children (unidentified)		12 East Street, Church Street
Mr Jordan		3 Walter's Terrace, Waller Street
Mrs Jordan		3 Walter's Terrace, Waller Street
Thomas White +one child	?	3 Walter's Terrace, Waller Street

Facts
It should be noted that Kaiser Wilhelm of Germany had expressly forbidden attacks upon civilian targets and housing, but the primitive navigational aids, erratic steering and crude bomb-sights of the Zeppelins meant that the airships often dropped bombs a long way from their intended targets.

[6] The original lists make it unclear whether this boy was killed or injured, but the totals given are correct if he was killed.

5/6 March 1916 (L 14 *Kptlt* Böcker, L 11 *Kvkpt* Schütze)

Killed (9)

Name	Age	Location and remarks
George Henry Youell	40	Queen Street
James Smith	30	2 Queen's Alley, Blackfriargate
Frank Cattle	8	50 Little Humber Street
Mira Lottie Ingamell	25	8 The Avenue, Linnaeus Street
Ethel Ingamell	?	8 The Avenue, Linnaeus Street
Martha Ingamell	?	8 The Avenue, Linnaeus Street
Edward Leadner	89	Trinity House Almshouses, Carr Lane
Edward Slip	45	23 Queen Street
James William Collinson	63	14 John's Place, Regent Street

Injured (12)

Name	Age	Location and remarks
Edwin Naylor	?	32 Collier Street
James Gallagher	?	30 Collier Street
Annie Beatty	?	24 Collier Street
Fred Beatty	?	24 Collier Street
Frank Johnson	?	22 Collier Street
Mrs Dees	?	Collier Street
Maggie Ellen Bournes	?	2 James Place, Collier Street
Frederick Cattle	?	50 Little Humber Street
Mrs Cattle	?	50 Little Humber Street
Mr Ingamell	?	8 The Avenue, Linnaeus Street
Mr Todd	?	5 The Avenue, Linnaeus Street
Mrs Todd	?	5 The Avenue, Linnaeus Street

9 August 1916 (L 24, *Kptlt* Koch)

Killed (10)

Name	Age	Location and remarks
Mary Louise Bearpark	44	35 Selby Street
Emmie Bearpark	14	35 Selby Street 'died from shock'
Rose Alma Hall	33	61 Selby Street (died 10/8/16)
Elisabeth Hall	9	61 Selby Street
Mary Hall	7	61 Selby Street (died 9/8/16)
John Charles Broadby	3	4 Roland Avenue, Arthur Street
Emma Louise Evers	46	Walliker Street (?)
Arthur Wilcockson	86	32 Granville Street 'died from shock'
Charles Linford	64	'died 14/8/16'
Elisabeth Jane Bond	76	6 Sydney Terrace, Grange Street; 'died from shock'

Injured (11)

Name	Age	Location and remarks
Albert Edward Bearpark	48	35 Selby Street
Wilfred Bearpark	12	35 Selby Street
William Hall	11	61 Selby Street
Minnie Tidball	11	62 Selby Street
John Edward Broadby	32	4 Roland Avenue, Arthur Street
Alice Maud Broadby	30	4 Roland Avenue, Arthur Street
Gertrude Louise Evers	40	25 Brunswick Avenue, St George's Road
Mary Alice Cherry	56	256 Division Road
Thomas Wilson	74	49 Sandringham Street
Ernest Horton	33	65 Sandringham Street
Sarah Horton	35	65 Sandringham Street

25 September 1917 (L 41, *Hptmn* Manger)

Injured (3)

Three women (unidentified)

12 March 1918 (L 63, *Kptlt* von Freudenreich)

Killed (1)

1 woman (unidentified) 'died from shock'

Total casualties from all raids:

44 killed

53+ injured

Incident
Although Hull endured air raid conditions at least seven times during the First World War, the city was only directly attacked as noted here. Other alarms were caused by the erratic paths followed by the Zeppelins as they entered and left British air space over the East Coast and Humber.
On 5 April 1916, Kvkpt Schütze in L 11 attempted to bomb Hull again, but was driven off by the newly-installed searchlights and anti-aircraft guns. Later that year, on 27 November, Hptmn Manger in L 41 tried to attack Hull, but was also driven away by gunfire. On his way home Manger dropped 44 bombs near Mappleton, causing no damage.

Sources and Bibliography

Sources

AIR 1 Public Record Office

DDBD90/119 East Riding of Yorkshire Council Archives

Minutes of Beverley Town Council for 1915 etc.

East Riding of Yorkshire Council Archives

Field Service Pocket Book April 1918, Royal Air Force Museum

List of Stations Royal Air Force Museum

Letter Wg Cdr W.E. Dunn to Colin Leadhill.

Hardcopy of *Training in the RFC* compiled from various sources
by H.C. Clark (C&C) and sent to the author during 2000.

6 Brigade RAF Mick Davis, International *Cross and Cockade Journal* Vol 30 No 2 1999

Documents relating to the Zeppelin raids on Hull, courtesy of Arthur Credland, Hull City Museums

Three aircraft typical of those used as advanced trainers in East Yorkshire is this group consisting of an Avro 504, SPAD VII and an Airco DH5 in the also typical muddy conditions found on Great War grass airfields.

Published Works

Action Stations No 4 (2nd Ed) B B Halpenny, PSL 1990

Aeroplanes of the Royal Aircraft Factory Paul R Hare, Crowood 1999

Airco Mick Davis, Crowood 2001

Airship Saga Lord Ventry, Blandford 1982

'Baby Killers', German Air Raids on Britain in the First World War Thomas Fegan, Pen & Sword 2002

Battlebags C Mowthorpe, Wrens Park 1998

Blackburn Aircraft since 1909 AJ Jackson, Putnam 1989

British Airfield Buildings Vol 2 G Buchan Innes, MCP 2000

British Military Aircraft Serials 1878-1987 B Robertson, MCP 1987

English Electric Aircraft and their Predecessors Ransom & Fairclough, Putnam 1987

Flying Units of the RAF Alan Lake, Airlife 1999

Howden Airship Station 1915-1921 T Asquith (Howden Civic Society Leaflet No 2)
    Icarus over the Humber TW Jamison, Lampada Press 1995

Luftschiffe Peter Meyer, Bernard & Graefe 1996

Military Airfield Architecture P Francis, PSL 1996

My Airship Days GF Meager, Kimber 1970

RAF Squadrons Wg Cdr CG Jefford, Airlife 1988

Royal Air Force Flying Training and Support Units Sturtivant, Hamlin and Halley, Air Britain 1997

Royal Navy Aircraft Serials & Units 1911-1919 R Sturtivant et al, Air-Britain 1992

Sopwith Aircraft Mick Davis, Crowood 1999

The Air Defence of Britain 1914-1918 Cole & Cheesman, Putnam 1984

The SE5 File Sturtivant & Page, Air-Britain 1996

The War in the Air Raleigh & Jones, Oxford University Press 1922-1937

White Rose Base B Rapier, Air Museum York 1980

Photographs

East Riding of Yorkshire Archives

Hull City Museums

Fleet Air Arm Museum

MG Simmons

JMB/GSL Collection

Barry Ketley

Maps and Site Plans

Steve Longland

Mick Davis

MG Simmons

Index

PEOPLE

The full range of Crécy Publishing books
including all Flight Recorder titles are
available online from www.crecy.co.uk
and from any bookshop

Crécy Publishing Limited
1a Ringway Trading Estate
Shadowmoss Road
Manchester M22 4LH

www.crecy.co.uk